2nd revised and expanded edition

9 Levels of Value Systems
a developmental model for personal growth
and the evolution of teams and organisations

Rainer Krumm

2nd revised and expanded edition

9 LEVELS
OF VALUE SYSTEMS

a developmental model for personal growth
and theevolution of teams and organisations

Rainer Krumm

Edition
CASTELLANUS

ISBN-13: 978-1721962426

Imprint
9 Levels of Value Systems | Eywiesenstraße 6 | 88212 Ravensburg | Germany
T +49 751 363 44 - 999 | F -739 | info@9levels.com | www.9levels.com

2nd revised and expanded edition 2018

Author: Rainer Krumm, 9 Levels Institute for value systems GmbH & Co. KG
Edition Castellanus
Design/typesetting: werdewelt.info
Illustrations: Timo Wuerz, www.timowuerz.com

Print: amazon CreateSpace

TABLE OF CONTENTS

Author's Preface – We're Ready for It!   8
Who is this Book for?   10

The Basics of the 9 Levels for Value Systems   11
The Origins of the Model   12

Three Perspectives of observation with the 9 Levels   15
Personal Value System   16
Group Value System   17
Organisation Value System   18

Overview of the 9 Levels   23

Basic Ideas of the 9 Levels   39

Value Systems and their Meaning   42

Coping Mechanisms   45
Reasons for Change   46

Model Dynamics   47
The Spiral Staircase – Stairway to Heaven?   47
The Model's Two Sides   48
The Model's Axioms   48
Specification of the levels according to
the order in the model   50

The Model's Levels   51
1st Level: Beige   51

2nd Level: Purple	53
3rd Level: Red	57
4th Level: Blue	62
5th Level: Orange	68
6th Level: Green	74
The First and the Second Tier	80
7th Level: Yellow	81
8th Level: Turquoise	87
9th Level: Coral	89
The Transfers between the Levels	90
Resistance to Value System	92
Change Management in the Model	100
Change Stages	102
Prerequisites for Change	103
Direction of Change in the Model	104
The 9 Levels in Practice	105
Cultural Change - Case	111
Areas of Application	117
Cultural change	117
Change processes	120
Individual coaching	123
Leadership	126
Outplacement/Placement	129
Recruiting	132
Team	135
Distribution/sales	138

**Stories Written by Life
– the 9 Levels are Among Us ...**   141

Thermals for the value systems   148

About the Author   154

References   156

AUTHOR'S PREFACE
We're Ready for It!

When I first came into contact with the research of Prof. Clare W. Graves in 2003, I was overwhelmed with the model's concurrent complexity and simplicity. The complexity of putting people, systems and the world into a dynamic model that is based on values and value systems is absolutely magnificent. I studied all the original sources of Prof. Graves that are still available. I evaluated audio and film documents and concretely applied them in consulting projects ever since. Christopher Cowan, one of the two authors of Spiral Dynamics and the guardian of Graves' legacy, trained me in South Africa.

Many models that work with persons, groups and organisations are static typologisations or analysis instruments focussing on behaviour. I found Graves' research fascinating because of its dynamics and depth reached by the focus on values. With my two co-authors and consultant colleagues, Martina Bär-Sieber and Hartmut Wiehle, I subsequently wrote the first German book on this theory. It was published under the title "Unternehmen verstehen, gestalten verändern – das Graves-Value-System in der Praxis". This book focuses on the application of Graves' theory to change processes in companies. It is a book with clear alignment of organisational development. In the meanwhile, further books for different fields have followed. In them, our "No.1" on the German market, which is deemed the reference book for Graves, is frequently cited. It thus also helped with the theory's breakthrough in our language area.

As consultant, management trainer and coach, I was still lacking a scientifically founded analysis tool. It had to be as pragmatic as suitable for practical use in consulting, training and coaching. Managers like to be guided by numbers. They give them the certainty they need for projects and decisions regarding employees and supervisors. Many executives and managers therefore are looking for something they can grasp and that is measurable. So I founded the "9 Levels Institute of Value Systems", pursuing the objective to offer tools for analysing value systems based on the research of Clare W. Graves. The 9 Levels of Value Systems were born: a further development of the Graves-Value-System, combined with the experiences from consulting and training people and companies in more than 23 different countries.

After more than 15 years of practical experience as a corporate consultant, management trainer and coach, the time to combine the many theoretical backgrounds with the knowledge and experience from practical use into one model had come. A model that can portray the dynamics and change of today's world and offer deeper explanation approaches than the previously common ones.

I wish all readers and users of the 9 Levels lots of fun, success and many new insights as they become intensely conscious of their own value systems.

It is time for new explanation approaches and models to successfully master the challenges of today's time.

Yours, Rainer Krumm

Contact: *info@9levels.com* | *www.9levels.com*

Who is this Book for?

This book is directed at people who come into contact with the Model of 9 Levels in seminars, workshops, consulting projects and coaching and who wish an intense and pragmatic introduction into the Model of 9 Levels, without having to work through the entire complexity of the underlying theory. It is intended to be an introduction that permits an understanding of the different levels, the model and its applications.

It is a book from practitioners for practitioners.

THE BASICS OF THE 9 LEVELS FOR VALUE SYSTEMS

The 9 Levels of Value Systems are targeted at persons, groups and organisations. It focuses on their development based on value systems.

In practice, this means that the Model of 9 Levels of Value Systems is used to illustrate the development of value systems or the target group. On the one hand, this is about being able to derive a better understanding for different manners of thinking and acting of persons, groups and organisations. On the other hand it helps to recognize necessary changes.

How does a person fit in a company? How does a department or deal suit the current tasks in the values guiding its actions? What challenges are posed by the environment/the market and how promising are the current value systems? Can current and future challenges be mastered with the current value consciousness and behaviour?

The 9 Levels model is a value meta model - a development model for personality development and evolution of organisations and cultures.

Values are the constitutive elements of culture. They define sense and meaning within a social system (group, society, etc.). Many models are targeted at persons' behaviour or unchangeable typologies. The model of 9 Levels goes deeper – it records the values. A value passed on by the culture serves as a "guideline" for people to understand or gain insights into the world. It thus becomes a premise for behavioural planning. The basic and action-controlling values are analysed and recorded. They control the manners of thinking, and the behaviour of persons, departments and organisations. They characterise corporate cultures, drive people, specify directions, provide the foundations of assessments, define what is right and wrong and contribute to a feeling of happiness and success depending on the degree to which they are met.

The Origins of the Model

The Model of 9 Levels is based on the insights of Clare W. Graves. Graves (1914 – 1986) was a professor of psychology at the Union College in New York (USA). In addition to his research work, he was a consultant of businesses, hospitals and educational institutions for many years. Graves got the idea for his research from his freshmen, who wanted to know which one of the many theorists (Maslow, Freud, Jung, Rogers, Watson, etc.) was right after all. Graves was unable to answer this question clearly. He wanted to find a way for this, however, and set out on a new research path. One of the central tasks in his research was the determination of the development stages of the human being. Upon asking his students to write a report describing the adult human being, he found that the descriptions were very different but contained recurring elements and systems. This brought him to the different development levels of human existence. A central task of his research was to understand these development levels of the human being.

He started to develop his theory in the 1950s. Christopher Cowan and Don Beck first published the model under the name Spiral Dynamics. Graves published his model in a Harvard Business Review article titled "Deterioration of Work Standards" in 1966. In this article, he called his model the "Levels of Human Behaviour". Later, Graves called his model/theory the "Emergent, cyclical double-helix model of adult biopsychosocial systems development". This model describes the differences in human development in a highly complex and multi-perspective manner. Graves' theory is an open model of value development. In different perspectives, it describes how people, systems and organisations see the world based on their biopsycho-social system.

Graves' approach combined elements of four different scientific disciplines: biology/neurobiology, psychology/theory of personality types, sociology/anthropology and system theory.

I wrote the first book on this basic model of the Graves-Value system in German in cooperation with Martina Bär-Sieber and Hartmut Wiehle, which was published in the Gabler Verlag in 2007. Under the title "Unternehmen verstehen, gestalten, verändern – das Graves-Value-System in der Praxis", it laid the foundation for this basic theory in the German speaking area. In the meantime, many books have been published on the different application options. They always refer to the basic model by Graves. The Graves-Value system is a value model that maps how individual or entire systems (departments, companies, organisations) think and act. It thus is a useful instrument for everyone working in or with organisations or teams and who wants to better understand them.

The development of the 9 Levels of Value Systems, by combining this theoretic model with a valid scientific analysis tool, was the logical consequence. The long experience with the model in consulting and coaching practice was contributed to this development. The demand is to combine the basic theory with the current research insights and references to the business world.

The 9 Levels are a simplification of Graves' theory, making it useful in a model for the development of people, groups and organisations.

The model of 9 Levels helps to better understand people, groups and organisations as well as their actions and reactions. The 9 Levels and the theory of value systems represent the dynamics responsible for development of individuals, groups and organisations. The value systems – also often referred to as psychological DNA – express mindsets, beliefs, internal states and organisational principles. The 9 Levels make them measurable and therefore also changeable.

THREE PERSPECTIVES OF OBSERVATION WITH THE 9 LEVELS

The Model of 9 Levels works for individuals as well as for teams and organisations. I will break down these three general approaches in more detail below.

Personal Value Systems

The Personal Value System analyses the individual and his or her value system. It focuses on one area of life. Depending on role and task, a person may use different value systems so that e-valuations and behaviour may change depending on the challenges of this specific part of his/her life.

An example: Paula Partner is department manager in a medium-sized, globally acting company that is specialised in semi-conductor electronics. She is responsible for global marketing and manages a department of 25 persons, 15 of which are working on site and 10 of which are distributed around the world. Her main contacts are the sales managers in the different global markets and regions. Privately, Paula Partner is married, has 2 children, aged three and seven. She works for UNICEF and is the parents' speaker in the kindergarten. She used to be a marketing expert in a small advertising agency that supported local customers quickly and individually. The first station in her career was that of a marketing trainee in a major corporation with a tradition of 125 years. Everything there was very well-ordered. In contrast, she perceived the advertising agency as too chaotic and fluctuating in workload. She is looking for another career change now. With the Personal Value Systems, the professional or role-specific value systems can now be analysed to see which corporate cultures or also which customers would suit her and where cooperation is going to work best.

Coaching is often able to use the Personal Value System to uncover and solve tension and fields of conflict.

Group Value Systems

Team development is the classic area of the Group Value System as a tool: What is the value system in a department or a project group? Which challenges of life does it have and wants to face? What should and has to be important for the members? Not every group is a team, and not all teams are sensible ones. How have the market and the tasks on it changed and which changes may be required because of this? How can this be described, designated and changed to permit sustainable value development?

An example: The sales organisation of a technical company working in special machinery construction was used to not actually having to engage in active sales due to their very high product quality. Instead, customers, as well as experts in the area, would ask if there were still any capacities left and whether the manufacturer was willing to make a machine for them. In the meantime, the competitor's quality has caught up and intense price pressure has resulted. The contacts are no longer the production managers, but usually purchasers and managers with little understanding of the technical aspect. Turnover strongly reduces and the employees in the sales department have no idea of why the old recipes and procedures no longer work. This is a classic case in which the model can help to recognise the necessary change. It shows why the once-successful approaches no longer work and no longer are successful.

Organisation Value Systems

The values and value systems of corporate culture or organisational culture are shared. Executives characterise them and are examples for the employees, who share them accordingly. This is a phenomenon of corporate culture that is difficult to grasp but can be recorded and measured with the Organisation Value System. Only this permits derivation of sustainable changes where necessary.

An example: A highly successful small company, initiated as a start-up, has developed a staff of 25 employees. Starting out with two founders as managing partners, the company grew to this size and three sites within only three years. The clear structure and controllability they were used to got lost. Subcultures develop in the sites. Holiday request forms and travel cost settlement forms have been established. The field service has fought with the office staff due to a lack of a clear strategy. The managers are so busy with day-to-day business that communication suffers there as well. The company wants to employ another 20 to 30 employees in the next years and establish an interim hierarchy. A previously intuitively managed start-up is "growing up", as one of the first employees smugly said.

The 9 Levels of Value System can analyse the current situation of the value systems of these three perspectives and determine the desired target condition of a person, group or organisation. Changing and adjustment to new situations is very important, specifically because everything around us, including people and systems, continually develops.

Coping-Mechanisms: The Interactions between the World and Value Systems

The world is not static. In particular, value systems are subject to development. Depending on the influences currently acting on a person from the outside and the inside, he will strive for change. His value systems will shift. To better understand a change, or to make this understanding possible in the first place, a dynamic model must be applied.

Of course, people and systems also mutually change their environment in interactions. Graves used this as a basis to derive the interaction between WORLD and REACTIONS. World and reactions mutually influence each other. The world changes the person and the person changes the world. He called the interactions "coping mechanisms", which I will deal with in more detail later on.

Man develops step by step, moving back and forth between I-centric and we-centric approaches, which is illustrated in this model as one side each. A new-born child automatically starts on the side of I-centricity on the lowest level "Beige". It is only interested in its basic needs for survival being met: It will cry when hungry or thirsty, tired or not feeling well. Groups and organisations begin their development comparably on the lowest level. Each additional step of development then leads upwards, similar to a spiral staircase, running through the levels shown below. From the most fundamental level "Beige", people move up to the top-most and perfectly I-centric level "Coral". Each new level includes the values of the previous ones on the way up. Levels cannot be skipped. As a child, each one first learns to sit and crawl in some manner before taking his or her first steps. In this context, the coping mechanisms express the change from one level to the next. Change usually also means conflict. In this context, present and established values are broken and developed further. Values that used to be common and manifested are changed or replaced. This change mechanism causes anxiety and results in an attempt to protect vested interests (power, material possessions, etc.).

PERSONAL value systems

9 LEVELS

GROUP value systems

9 LEVELS

ORGANISATION value systems

9 LEVELS

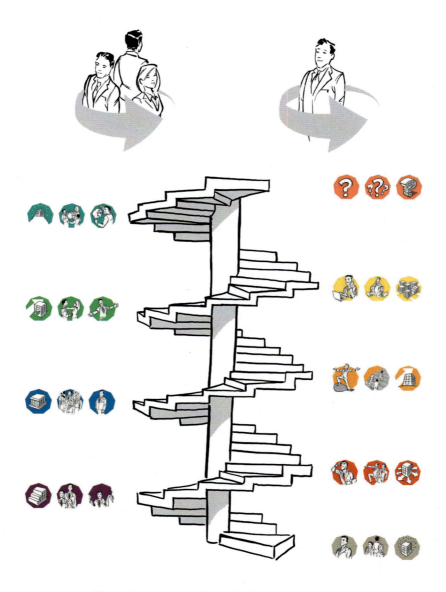

Figure 1: overview of the 9 levels of value systems

OVERVIEW OF THE 9 LEVELS

Below, I will present the basic ideas of the 9 levels and then deal with them in more detail. Levels 1 to 6 are the first-tier levels. These first 6 levels react to deficit needs in one's own life. From the second tier onwards, the levels repeat on a higher stage, with a focus on sense and meaning.

LEVEL BEIGE

On the 1st level, people are at the most fundamental level of life and consciousness. They live in small groups or clans that offer a certain degree of protection and help secure their basic needs, such as food, water, heat and procreation. Beige is driven by instinct and acts intuitively. Primal fear of loss of the strength needed to survive is his companion. In business, this level is fighting for economic survival. The Beige level is not part of the applied tool and as such not being measured.

LEVEL PURPLE

On the 2nd level, people see themselves as part of a community, a clan, a tribe, with a patriarch or chief as leader. The clan offers protection, safety and a place to belong to. Everything is going according to a set of rules that is specified – usually not put in writing – and that is not questioned. Sacrifice and obedience are required. Purple has a magically-mystic consciousness. Traditions and customs are maintained, and superstition has its place as well. In the business environment, these are often patriarchal family companies with few functional structures.

Characteristic values are:

- » Tradition
- » Blood relationship
- » Customs
- » Passing on traditions
- » Homeland
- » Rituals
- » Respecting taboos
- » Obedience
- » Security
- » Magically-mystic consciousness
- » Protection
- » Willingness to sacrifice
- » Commitment
- » Hospitality
- » Archaic-magical yearnings
- » Belonging
- » Habit
- » Securing existence
- » Harmony

LEVEL RED

On the 3rd level, people consider themselves to be conquerors and rulers over new areas. They strive for power, independence and renown. Resources are used for their own benefit. In doubt, people will act without taking into account the losses. Red can take initiative quickly – and often act powerfully and innovatively. Rules and laws are not known to or wanted by him. The stronger person will prevail. Markets of conquest or harsh structural sales companies fall into this category. They are targeted at their own benefits – without taking anything else into account.

Characteristic values are:

- » Assertiveness
- » Power
- » Courage
- » Self-confidence
- » Prestige (respect, awe, fear)
- » Honour
- » Aggression
- » Strength
- » Impulsiveness
- » Dominance
- » Independence
- » Conquest, e.g. of new markets
- » Demand for respect
- » Presence-oriented, egocentric, concrete thinking
- » Bravery
- » Personal success
- » Winning at any cost
- » Self-admiration
- » Avoiding "shame"

LEVEL BLUE

On the 4th level, people are looking for rules and laws. They consider themselves to be part of a system of order. This points out clear structures and responsibilities according to which life and action works. Justice is highly valued and expected. Loyalty is regarded. Blue is characterised by a high degree of diligence and discipline. Identity is gained through the collective. Hierarchies are emphasized. Job descriptions are important and rules as well as structures are introduced.

Characteristic values are:

- » Duty
- » Quality
- » Law and order
- » Discipline
- » Guilt and innocence
- » Stability
- » Loyalty
- » Order
- » Reliability
- » Control
- » Truth
- » Patience
- » Compliance with rules
- » Rank / Status
- » Clarity
- » Compliance with hierarchies
- » Justice
- » Safety
- » Titles

LEVEL ORANGE

On the 5th level, people always focus on their own success to maintain and increase their wealth. They have lots of energy and act in a targeted fashion. They are looking at things as a whole. Their success will not always be at the expense of someone else. Orange is characterised by further development with a clear target orientation and a continuous, rapid increase of performance. He is restless. Cooperation is characterised by process orientation and target agreements.

Characteristic values are:

- » Performance
- » Prestige (status symbols)
- » Responsibility
- » Personal success + overall success
- » Status / status symbols
- » Career orientation
- » Competition
- » Productivity
- » Target orientation
- » Profit orientation
- » Process orientation
- » Result orientation
- » Wealth
- » Challenge
- » Entrepreneurial thinking
- » Independence
- » Acceptance
- » Focus
- » Value generation
- » Monetary and economic growth

LEVEL GREEN

On the 6th level, people consider success to be the result of the correct team configuration. Their thinking is aligned with achieving objectives – but in combination with team thinking, mutual action and formation of a consensus. The objective is long-term mutual securing of success. Meetings, persons and relationships are more important to him than the cause. Green is in a continuous dialogue with his environment. As compared to Blue and Orange, Green is thinking less in absolutes but rather weighing different opinions against each other. For him, there are several books, rather than one book. Terms such as participation and integration are important terms for him in cooperation.

Characteristic values are:

» Cooperation
» Open-mindedness (towards the entire world)
» Tolerance
» Harmony
» Consensus
» Responsibility for the other
» Dialogue
» Integration (of people)
» Empathy
» Participation
» Equality
» Appreciation
» Fairness
» Human rights
» Adaptation
» commonality / community
» Ensuring long-term success
» Personal and human growth

This was the last level in the first tier. From here onwards, the second tier begins, where the levels repeat, but on a higher stage. The focus is now on sense and meaning.

LEVEL YELLOW

On the 7th level, people are first able to understand, use and combine the benefits of the levels that have come before. The second tier results: The previous levels have only considered the world and its understanding from their own perspective. This multi-perceptivity was closed to them. For Yellow, the focus is on increasing knowledge, flexibility, competence and independence. Material possession, power and status are secondary. Yellow thinks in multiple perspectives and systematically, as well as with great abstraction skills. Networking and changing cooperation are a matter of course. Rank and status are unimportant. He focuses on competence and knowledge. Yellow is the Beige of the second tier.

Characteristic values are:
- » Individuality
- » Self-reflection
- » Multi-perspectivity
- » Systemic integration
- » Knowledge
- » Creativity
- » Personal development
- » Integration
- » Self-responsibility
- » Networking
- » Life-long learning
- » Appreciation of uniqueness
- » Vision
- » Autonomy
- » Profound competence
- » Active growth (mental / knowledge)
- » Integration (of knowledge)
- » Open-mindedness (towards other opinions and knowledge / poly-contextural logic)
- » Innovation

LEVEL TURQUOISE

Man on the 8th level acts only towards sustainability and holistically. Turquoise is thinking holistically-global, ecologically and intuitively. He focuses on the world's welfare and aligns his life and work with it. In his altruistic attitude, he may be observer as well as designer. Turquoise is the second-tier Purple.

Characteristic values are:
- » Sustainability
- » Holon (the whole as part of another whole)
- » Responsibility for the future of life
- » Systemic action
- » Acceptance of global complexity
- » Improvement of living conditions for all life forms
- » Entrepreneurial responsibility for society
- » Social and ecological sense and general context
- » Collective intuition
- » Nature-orientation
- » Spiritual awareness for the benefit of humanity
- » High ideals
- » Global reconciliation
- » Self-organisation of living systems
- » Farsightedness
- » Network intelligence

LEVEL CORAL

On the 9th level, people are the second-tier Reds. They are egocentric and live with the knowledge that there are no limits that are not generated by human action and being. Filled with love and respect for all living beings, Coral motivates people to take new paths and to exceed limitations with his charisma. Like the 1st level, the 9th level is not directly part of the developed system and therefore is also not being measured.

THE BASIC IDEAS OF THE 9 LEVELS

The model describes systems in persons, groups and organisations, rather than systems of people and organisations. It is not a typology. It is about seeing the "why" behind the behaviour. Why is someone able to deal with the specific value systems of other levels better, less well, or not at all? This requires that this person, group or organisation understands the current internal value system and the level of consciousness, as well as any changes of environment or on the market and understands how things need to be adjusted. The 9 levels help in understanding other value orientations. They convey the knowledge required to initiate necessary change.

The 9 Levels have 3 basic principles:
» Persons, groups and organisations go through development stages. They are always the same and based on each other.
» Change has certain prerequisites. Without them, change is not possible. These 7 prerequisites of ability and willingness are described later.
» There are so-called supporting variables which persons, groups and organisations can be helped with in the change process.

Typical principles for working with the 9 Levels:
» "The solutions of yesterday are today's problems; the solutions of today are tomorrow's problems."
» "The complexity of thinking has to surpass the complexity of the problem."
» "In the end, more complex thinking will prevail over less complex thinking because it permits higher degrees of detail when

handling changed circumstances."

» "Everyone has the right to be as they are. Teach people to improve the quality of their work by meeting their manners of thinking and not using yourself as a basis."

» "People should not have to change too much to do their work. Use them according to their own strengths."

» "Make change easier and support those who want to change. Do not punish the others for being and wanting to remain what they are."

Areas of Use for the Model

The Model of 9 Levels of Value Systems is the basic model to explain and map value systems of persons, groups and organisations.

As indicated above, many people have difficulties grasping the value systems. To make them measurable in the future, we at 9 Levels have developed 3 analysis tools with scientific assistance. The tools that have proven their worth in consulting, coaching and training practice have thus been scientifically verified.

Generally, the central model of 9 Levels has three perspectives - or three pairs of glasses - to observe and analyse value systems, each in the ACTUAL and from case to case also in the desired TARGET situation. The model is used in:

Personal Value System – focussing on the person
» Individual coaching
» Outplacement
» Placement
» Recruiting / Assessment Center

- » Career consulting
- » Executive coaching
- » Young executive development

Group Value System – focussing on the group / team
- » Team development
- » Team coaching
- » Executive development
- » Sales optimisation
- » Process optimisation

Organisation Value System – focussing on the organisation
- » Corporate culture change
- » Interface optimisation
- » Organisation development
- » Change management

VALUE SYSTEMS AND THEIR MEANING

Why Are Values (Value Systems) Important?

Everyone needs values for orientation and support. Values subconsciously determine our actions. They tell us whether something is good or bad, whether we accept or reject something, how we should or should not behave in situations and so on. Values are our constant companion in all situations in life.

- » Values drive people.
- » Values indicate direction.
- » Values are the foundation for evaluation. What is right and what is wrong?
- » Values met make us happy and successful.
- » Accordingly, values not met make us unhappy and unsuccessful.

Using this insight, we can very nicely illustrate the influence of values and value systems on our actions regarding the model of 9 Levels. Many models approach the behaviour of persons or typologies that cannot be changed. The model of 9 Levels goes deeper because it analyses and records the value and is able to provide a comprehensive insight into how people, departments and organisations work and how corporate cultures are characterised. The values that apply for the different levels are listed in the respective explanations in the chapter "The Model's Levels".

Not only does every person have different values that are essential for him or her, the ranking of the individual values also differs. One may put particular store in living in harmony even if this means keeping back with his or her own interests. Another may consider reaching the target he has set for himself to be of top priority, even if this is at the expense of others. Each one of us also has a different "understanding of values", which means that a value can be interpreted very differently by different persons. For example, the value "honesty" may mean always being honest and authentic towards others for one, while others consider it an opportunity of representing their own position without compromises. Values therefore determine how we see the world, what we believe in and what we perceive to be good or bad.

Beliefs and values are drivers and inhibitors of our skills at the same time.

In the interhuman context, different value ideas are an ideal basis for difficulties and conflict. Any person will also experience inner conflict when acting or being forced to act against his or her own values. Looking at these two aspects, we can see that values are not only important for the creation and escalation of crisis, but that they are also the central requirement for dealing with the strain.

Value systems can also turn lighter or darker when the living situation changes. Every person has a "dimmer" that permits adjusting the "brightness" of the value system, depending on changes in the environmental conditions. The "pure form" of a value system is nearly non-existent. The levels as we use them are the strongest versions of the value systems. People can be on different levels in different areas of life or situations. The performance-oriented Orange manager may be deeply Blue in his family and perfectly Red when looking for the high of base jumping.

Value systems and consciousness:

We assume that when a person is aware of a situation or condition, he or she will perceive this situation and think about it. Consciousness, first of all, is a function of the psychophysical, the perception organs, the brain. With reason, people try to explain their perception - by looking at the outside of something or turning their attention to inner processes to explain what they are. This is done by human consciousness, which has several areas and may in turn be part of different steps of consciousness.

Level of Consciousness
= steps of consciousness
= stage of consciousness

The level of consciousness is characterised by specific value attitudes / value hierarchies / value systems. If the living situation changes in a specific area, the person (unconsciously) switches to a different level of consciousness in this area on which he or she will try to find a solution for the situation. It is possible that the person has several well-developed levels and switches between the levels regarding situation. This is also referred to as the coping mechanisms that I have mentioned before and will deal with in more detail below.

Value-Mix – Nothing is Absolute

No person, no group and no organisation has a unique value system – rather, it is a mix of current and previous values and their interrelations and systems, as is made clear in the comparison with a dimmer in a light switch. Like the lights can be on on several floors in a building, several levels of the model can apply. Moving on to the next level usually means dimming down the previous value systems a little and turning up the light on the current floor more brightly.

COPING MECHANISMS

"No one can solve problems by thinking in the manner that caused them."
Albert Einstein

Because our world is subject to continuous change, we as people also have to continually re-orient and adjust. This applies for systems as well. Of course, this holds true vice versa as well, since continuous adjustment and changes in ourselves will influence our environment. Everything - the world and we in it with our actions - are therefore in a continuous interrelationship. Everything causes a reaction. Graves calls these interrelationships the "coping mechanisms".

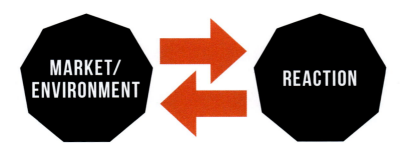

These coping mechanisms are the changes from one level to the next. Every level includes the values of the previous one in this process. Since every change usually includes necessary changes or even loss of what is familiar and proven, conflicts are a foregone conclusion. People undergoing this kind of change are haunted by fears of loss of power, prestige, possessions and so on.

"The problem is not in finding new ideas, but in escaping from the old ones."
Baron Keynes

Reasons for Change

Which reasons are such triggers? What causes change – or a coping mechanism? Both in personal respect and in groups and organisations, change may be diverse. Value systems do not suddenly change. Rather, they are slow processes that will at times symbolically erupt. The value system has already changed. The decisive trigger point is pushed somewhere along the way afterwards.

For people, this may be the loss of a long-term job or taking up a new position, having a new family member, losing a beloved person, a consequential diagnosis and so on. For groups, this may be new tasks and provisions, a new supervisor, different compensation processes or a failed project.

In organisations, this may be changes in the management, such as a generation change, loss of an important customer, restructuring, new executives with new approaches or different process and structural organisation.

In companies, this may be economic development, the creation of new parties or a change in the government, severe disasters such as Fukushima, a health reformation or a financial crisis – to name just a few reasons for change.

No matter the type of the change, we usually face it fearfully and sceptically, which influences how we deal with the changes that are needed. Will we vehemently try to refuse? Will we passively resist? Are we going to be able to fight fears and scepticism? Are companies able to reduce fears, reservations and insecurities among their employees? Every action will lead to a corresponding reaction.

MODEL DYNAMICS

Everything around us is in motion. In particular, the value systems are subject to development in this. Depending on the influences from the outside and inside on a person, this or that change will happen, causing in turn an adjustment of the person's value systems. Therefore, it is important to use a dynamic model that can adjust to new situations just as we and our environment do, to be better able to understand and permit change. The 9 levels "spiral staircase" makes just this possible.

The Spiral Staircase - Stairway to Heaven?

On a spiral staircase, you are continually in motion. There is no platform to rest on. Even if we seem to "rest" on a level, we are still in motion, moving on in our development. The model of 9 Levels with its spiral staircase structure illustrates this continuous further development of our values very nicely, showing the entire dynamics and complexity in this system.

Every level has its justification, depending on the framework conditions that the environment poses to the person, the group or the organisation. It is not about quickly moving higher and farther or being better. Rather, it is about seeing whether the value systems match the challenges of life. It is no "stairway to heaven".

The Model's Two Sides

The model has two sides on the spiral staircase, comparable to the central staircase in a building. The left side is the **WE-centric**

side. People on this side want the group or organisation they are part of to be well while putting themselves second. We-centricity is characterised by orientation in a group of individuals. People are willing to contribute to the community and do not expect personal benefit or added value right away. This is also described as "sacrifice now – reward later": Contributions are made now, but the incentive / reward may only occur later. People try to adjust to the environment.

The right side is very different from this. These are persons who first and foremost think of their own well-being and are very strongly self-focussed. This is the **I-centric** side. I-centricity is aligned with the individual and personal interests. People try to adjust the environment to themselves.

The Model's Axioms

» The model of 9 Levels of Value Systems describes how people / systems think, rather than how they are. It explains why systems/ people act this or that way.

» All levels of the model are entirely equal in value. None are worse or better. They merely need to match their environment.

» Every new level results from reactions to the previous levels.

» Development moves from bottom up. Levels cannot be skipped.

There is no elevator in this building!
» Top levels imply lower ones. Complexity increases.

An Important Aspect When Using the Model:
» Always ask "why" someone does something, not "what" they do!
» The model is a development model rather than a typology! It describes systems in people (companies or systems), rather than types of people (companies or systems).

I have already generally described the levels above. In the following statements, I will take up general examples from daily life and then additionally focus the levels on the three analysis tools Personal Value System, Group Value System and Organisation Value System.

Specification of the levels according to the order in the model

You have already got to know the general description of the levels. In the following, I will take up general examples from everyday life and directly focus the levels on the three analysis tools Personal Value System, Group Value System and Organisation Value System.

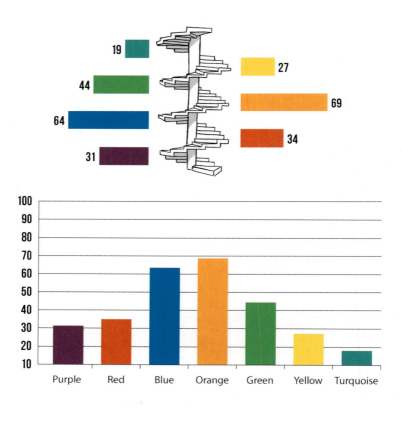

THE MODEL'S LEVELS

1st Level: Beige

A new-born starts on the Beige level. Initially, he will only be interested in pure survival. Once he tries to find explanations for the world and creatures such as Santa Clause, the Easter Bunny or the Tooth Fairy appear, the level Purple has been reached. Soon, the child will want to enforce his own interests and the phase of defiance appears. He will insist on getting what he wants. In the sand box, he will ruthlessly and sometimes forcefully defend his shovel. If the parents establish an anti-authoritarian upbringing now, they close off the path into Blue. A child who experiences and leads no rules or order can hardly develop into Blue, leading to great problems when the child enters a Blue system such as school.

1st Level: Beige Personal

Beige is the level of "wanting to survive". Life is centred on securing survival.

The 1st level is characterised by primarily being about the survival of the individual. Human and biological needs for food, water, warmth and safety are at the focus and determine the course of the day. The body determines what is needed. The environment greatly influences people on the 1st level. Climate conditions, food stores and hostile dangers from other beings in the area characterise this value. People live from what their environment offers. Reactions are often reactive and similar to reflexes. People live with the primal fear of loss of powers required for survival. They have no perception of space and time yet. They live in the here and now. However, Beige has the intuition of perceiving other dimensions of time and space that have been nearly completely lost to highly developed people, as can be seen when highly civilised persons suffer nature disasters or are invited to survival camps. Senses are very keen.

Persons characterised by Beige on the 1st level know no organised forms of life or special systems. The body decides what is needed to survive. Habits and instinctive behaviour ensures survival. The battle is the driving force. These people are said to have foresight or a 7th sense because their thinking is limited to what is essential and currently relevant.

Beige thinking and actions today are regressive conditions that will disappear again but may occur after severe accidents, disease, psychological trauma or old-age dementia. There are still some small groups of indigenous people who live in stone-age structures with strong Beige influences. It may also occur in individual situations, e.g. when losing sensual perception due to being drunk or under the influence of drugs. On the 1st level, man is egocentric and I-centric.

1st Level: Beige Group

The group in Beige is a small, loose network that has no organisational structures. The group considers itself part of nature and is only established to survive and procreate. The senses of the individual members are strongly developed, which is important for the daily fight for survival. The non-verbal communication skills within the group make quick re-action to danger possible based on instinct. Since Beige is I-centric, every member will try to survive alone within the group.

1st Level: Beige Organisation

A Beige level organisation cannot exist. Beige is the most fundamental level of consciousness and as such unable to form social systems or organised forms of life. The higher-developed value systems will usually prevail even if companies suffer situations that threaten their existence.

2ⁿᵈ Level: Purple

The purple level marks the beginning of cooperation with, but also differentiation from others. Everyone feels to be part of a community and without it he or she cannot survive. In the community they look out for supernatural explanations in order to leave their fear and lack of power behind and to become mighty. A magical way of thinking prevails.

2ⁿᵈ Level: Purple Personal

This is the level of the ancestors, the group, family, clan, and today it is the level of associations, networks, patriarchally managed small enterprises.

On the Purple level, people see themselves as part of a social system, similar to a family member. The family or system provides protection, shelter and thus the important feeling of belonging. The Purple person does not mind that his rules are determined by others. Quite the opposite: He feels well taken care of and very comfortable.

A person who rules a social system also considers himself responsible towards his members. In this role, he will care for them as well as exercise authority over them. He never questions his decisions and actions, but considers his predominant situation to be perfectly legal. The hierarchy below him is clearly structured and his successors have been determined in advance. The followers adore this "head stallion" and would never question his authority. After all, he is the only one whose power can protect them from dangerous situations and attacks from the outside. It is important to him as a leader to learn what the individual members of his group consider important. The final decision, however, is entirely up to him.

People on the Purple level increasingly think with the right half of their brains. They are very visually characterised and have a stronger consciousness for body and space. The right half of the brain combines many impressions into an overall image. Seeing dark clouds collect in the sky, and unconsciously also perceiving the changed barometric pressure, a smell of rain, rising wind and the first lightning in the distance, we know that it is time to find a dry place. On the Purple level, this perception is accordingly strengthened while people on other levels may have to get wet before they even realise that a thunderstorm is threatening. Purple is a pioneer in all areas of creativity and emotion. He loves people who stand out by special skills, e.g. by a particularly well-developed type of perception. He connects everything that has happened before to experience, the people and places involved. The time at which this happened, the month or year, is not relevant for him. As known by indigenous peoples, Purple persons believe in the higher powers of nature, spirits and the power of souls of the dead. They will perform rites to honour the superhuman powers and mollify them with sacrifices. In the civilised world, this level assigns high importance to family rituals, traditions and society.

Persons on the Purple level are perfectly comfortable in their role and the connected tasks and work as part of a group. They enjoy being needed and cut back on their own needs for this. This absolute we-centricity makes it impossible for people to leave their determined rules. If the leader commands a change, however, it is accepted silently. Personal values are identification, solidarity, willingness to sacrifice and traditions. All in all, dependence on the group is very high.

2nd Level: Purple Group

On the Purple level, the focus is clearly on the group, as is expressed by the we-centricity. If the environment poses many demands, the group faces them as one. The most important thing is to ensure the existence and survival of the group. The clear structure within this system ensures that everyone has a role with specific tasks.

The tasks, however, are usually so complex that they could not be assumed by anyone else. Men and women hold classic roles. The group leader makes the final decision on who assumes which task. He may seem solidly united with his group members but makes the decisions on his own in the end, which the group fully accepts.

The members of level Purple use symbols, just like the individual knight clans in the Middle Ages did to differentiate themselves from the others. Clear association is communicated as well as the pride every individual feels in being part of this group. The latter is connected to a high degree of dependence. On the one hand, the group is extremely strong by this strong perception of belonging together, but on the other hand, any new member of the group is a vulnerability of the system and may weaken it. One can only be fully a part of the group or be isolated.

All peoples have Purple roots. Some still live in tribes, but even modern societies still reflect Purple in traditions and rituals, e.g. on local festivals. Unfortunately, Purple level groups are only mentioned negatively at the moment: Ethnical conflict such as the war in Bosnia and other racist violence often have Purple roots.

2nd Level: Purple Organisation

Companies on the Purple level usually have just a few employees and are controlled by a manager who acts as the patriarch. This includes family-owned operations managed by one family member only. Customers of these small companies are usually individuals or other small companies. The company is very regionally aligned, with the region offering a secure purchaser for the goods produced or services sold. It is very important that everything is aligned with each other in a very harmonious fashion.

The manager's expectations to the employees are comparable to the situation of last century's small operations: Identification with the employer is expected as well as absolute loyalty and sacrifice. The employees are strongly integrated into what happens in the company, but the leader's word is the law here as well. His final decisions are not questioned. The well-being and security of employees is as important to him as ensuring continuation of the operation as such. Measures that must be performed to implement this are not determined or put in writing anywhere. They are simply based on a matter of course.

The hierarchy in a Purple company is structured in no more than two levels, with the patriarch on top and the second level with fined structures and a fixed area of tasks for every single employee below. Although other employees would follow in lower hierarchy levels, they have no defined tasks. This is where people are deployed according to qualification. Then when the entire organisation has more people, the undefined bottom level will also have clear responsibilities assigned, e.g. for purchasing.

It is also not important for Purple organisations to become market leaders in an area. Only maintenance of the current position is important. Small inns, restaurants or crafts operations are among these organisations.

3rd Level: Red

On the Red level, everything is about power, renown and pure personal benefit. Rules don't matter. Laws aren't needed. The winner is he who races forward without any concern for loss. A Red bank employee, for example, may steal a DVD with data from a Blue Swiss bank and offer it to the German state because it contains tax evader data. The Blue legal system, which will be dealt with next, then says that it first needs to review whether this material may be legally bought or whether it is classified as stolen after all, in which case it would not be permitted to buy it in spite of permitting to find red tax evaders or orange tax optimisers. The orange perspective that I will deal with later tends to consider what the data would cost and whether the transaction would be profitable. After all, a Red tax fraudster will gladly demand the moral decency of treating him Blue. Other Oranges will wonder whether the existence of the file may be a rumour to begin with. Or did the feint cause enough tax evaders to self-report already?

3rd Level: Red Personal

People on the Red level are egocentric, self-confident and hard-working while they are working for their own success. They make impulsive decisions and trust only in their skills, the opportunities of the moment and the effect of their strong personalities on others. In the presence of a group, they consider themselves of higher rank and expect to be respected, minded and admired by others. They do not care about the group as such, except where they need it for their personal benefit. A "Red" is unable to even imagine having to subject himself to others in any manner. It is particularly important to him to secure the position he has conquered. It must not be destroyed by slander or any scandals. He does everything in his own explosive interest. He acts contrary to the evolution theory of Charles Darwin "survival of the fittest", probably living according to "survival of the strongest" instead. If this theory helps him develop his position even further, he will feel that he has the right of things and be satisfied. If something does not work as expected, it will, of course, be exclusively the fault of the others, or the conditions just weren't right. Red would never look to himself for reasons. He cannot admit to having made any errors.

The I-centric Red thinks and acts in the present only. He never considers the consequences of his actions for tomorrow. Taking precautions for old-age pension or in medical respect are minor things for him that do not match his manner of thinking. He would never commit to anything that he does not believe to be a direct benefit for him.

The characteristics of a Red person can be positively as well as negatively aligned. A positive Red person will inspire people by his or her vivid and edifying manner. Others will like to stay around this Red person because they can be sure to never be bored here. There will always be surprises in store. A negatively aligned person will lead to people keeping their distance because they know that there is a risk of them being harmed. If you have to work with a person characterised by Red in business, never forget the benefits he will take from the business relationship. Someone who tries to threaten a person on the Red level will most likely end up as the loser.

Looking for Red people today, we will mainly find them among extreme athletes: Fun, action, the here and now is what counts, the high or just showing, "Look - I'm the greatest!" All in all, persons aligned with Red find it difficult to live out their characterisation in our civilised time. If you cannot fit into society well, you will always experience conflict because your difference is noticed. This is not always positive. Red teens, for example, cannot wait to leave their parents' home and go looking for new challenges. They may even run off all of a sudden because there are a lot more exciting and new things to discover without the parents' custody. Others hide in cyber worlds and seek to break out of the system they perceive as restricting in this manner. They are not clear about which consequences their behaviour has on their further development - only the here and now counts.

Thinking back, Red people used to be much better able to live their inclinations. There was so much left to conquer and discover. Just think of the colonial masters, who often brutally exploited the local peoples and wanted to force their own ideas onto them.

3rd Level: Red Group

In a Red group, nearly anyone may be or become the leader if he is egoistic enough and does not look right or left on the way there. Below the leader, there is a power hierarchy that has been determined in battle. Everyone keeps having to defend his or her position so that there is a constant situation of fighting for power within the group, with no one caring for whether the opponent may take damage or not, just as long as they defend their own position successfully or even move up a little more. The leader self-confidently observes these internal fights for the individual positions and may even spur them on.

The only reason for being part of a group is that it secures one's own well-being and existence. People will leave the group if the slightest doubt occurs that these conditions are still present. This may, of course, lead to the entire group dissolving. Persistence and seeming fairness are only short in their duration. If they persist at all for a while, they are very unstable and often subject to bribes. All in all, the I-centricity is very prominent within the group and acts highly counterproductively for this kind of constellation: Usually, the individual members of a group are supposed to be there for each other, support and strengthen each other. Red groups, however, are built on a very unstable foundation. If anyone no longer sees any benefit for himself, he will leave.

Red groups include city gangs, drug cartels, revolutionary groups, sports teams or strongly sales-oriented industries with structural sales.

3rd Level: Red organisation

Companies on the Red level can be found where new markets open up or a leading position on a market that has become crowded is to be achieved. The task of such organisations is in always reaching the objective set, no matter the cost. Such companies mainly focus on cost-efficient mass production of goods or services that do not require great investments. They want to be the unbeatable market leader here and prevail with cheap offers.

It is particularly important for these companies to be and remain independent. With the right leader, who is fully respected and minded by his employees, this target is also fully secured. There is a strong feeling of wanting to belong and being able to draw one's own benefit from this by holding the corresponding position. The knowledge of having power over others is also a strong driver for performance within the Red enterprise. If errors have happened in a hierarchy level, everything is done to hide them. After all, errors or deficits are connected to a mistake of the corporate management, which will ensure that the perpetrator will not get away unscathed. Vehemently strengthening and defending his position is important at all times for the leader of a Red enterprise. He is always subject to threatening attacks both from the inside and the outside. If you are familiar with the internal workings of this system, however, nothing keeps you from achieving all you wish.

Just like Purple, there are no written strategies or long-term and sustainable objectives here. Everyone knows what to do. The principle is achieving a quick turnover, a powerful position on the market and fast growth.

A company on the Red level often has many employees who can be quickly and easily replaced. In the hierarchic structure, every manager has his own staff of employees who perform similar tasks as compared to others on their level and thus also can be exchanged among each other.

The manager draws personal benefit from cooperation and exploits the "subordinates", but also lets them participate in the happenings within the company. The employees thus feel involved and as part of the company because they pursue the same objectives as their boss. People always know what their supervisor thinks because he will directly reward or punish any action.

Companies on the Red level are characterised by speed, quick reaction and assertiveness. The companies achieve this through their Red managers who have turned the organisation into what it currently is. A manager who skilfully uses his employees and thus supports the company's executive level well will be seen as having earned his position and can continue to use it for his own benefit.

It is not necessary for entire organisations to be Red. In some, e.g. Blue companies, "Red sheep" have formed that have brought a great number of people to the brink of ruining their existence because they were only caring for their personal benefit. Small groups of bankers who caused the financial crisis in 2008 are one recent example. Wholly Red organisations are mainly found on new markets on which they establish and secure a predominant position right away.

4ᵗʰ Level: Blue

The 4th level is the level of order, rules and laws. In it, people are looking for structure and clear requirements and consider themselves to be part of this system of order. As the system's name says, order-based structures are predominant. To be part of it, one has to naturally submit to them. As expected, justice being lived here in a distinctive way is presumed. Honesty is supported as well as rewarded. Blue persons are diligent and decent. They are most comfortable in a group.

When fresh deep snow is beckoning with outstanding snow conditions in winter, Blue mountain railways operators will often (and surely rightfully so) put up warning and prohibition signs to keep skiers and free riders from taking risks - also to exclude any risk of liability. I once saw a rather Blue skier standing in front of this kind of prohibition sign on a "powder day" like this, contemplating the risk and finally deciding: "Come on! We'll go in there anyway, won't we?"

4ᵗʰ Level: Blue Personal

On this level, we will find people who love order and are strongly aligned with law, loyalty and truth. The provisions, laws and responsibilities here give people the support and protection they so strongly crave. Of course, the entire organisation is accepted without question. A specific distribution of work determines who takes which tasks, with hierarchies among each other being observed without having to be afraid that someone might saw off the branch you are sitting on.

On the Blue level, people place great store in meeting their obligations and keeping their work in the usual level. They want to be perfectly honest and truthful towards third parties and be able to identify with a group particularly strongly. The community as such gives them the safety they need to survive. To feel well taken care of in the community, they will gladly sacrifice their own interest and adjust to the general population instead. We-centricity is extremely strong here, because Blue people intently focus on their group and its values, which is also reflected to the outside, e.g. in an association, by engaging in a mutual hobby, in a department and among the boy scouts. This strong sense of belonging is also often outwardly presented in the form of symbols or uniforms. Icons or clothing may indicate the association one belongs to or the hierarchy within the group.

The latter is particularly important because it firmly defines a clear responsibility that offers safety towards one's area of tasks. Absolute transparency does not permit any ambiguities to arise. A Blue employee needs his specific job description and is proud of his tasks. He will try to avoid problems and instead move along the provisions and rules. He always wants to do "the right thing". If he has done his job well, he will rejoice in the praise. If he fails, his feeling of guilt will be so strong that he will accept his punishment without complaint. Blue people think in old patterns and rather "conventionally", but also in a determined and precise manner. The supervisor's word is law. Status is important.

The Blue level also has negative and positive characterisations. Negatively characterised persons lack tolerance, are narrow-minded, take ages for coming to a decision, are subject to forces they have imposed on themselves and tend to pose strict requirements of themselves. People with this characterisation often draw others to themselves who "want to belong". Anyone not joining them is automatically deemed the enemy who refuses to observe the rules of this group. Other opinions are wrong and not tolerated. This behaviour can nearly be compared to that of missionaries who want to force their belief on others.

People with a positive alignment are very stable and have a high sense of responsibility. For them, it is important that laws and rules are complied with and the well-being of all is warranted. All they do is well-structured, diligent and very well organised. You can absolutely rely on their word. Supervisors are comfortable around them because they are attentive, honest and polite employees. People with a positive Blue characterisation live with their values, which give their lives meaning and structure at once.

Large companies with conservative management styles are often found on the Blue level. Representatives of this alignment are found on all levels of hierarchy. Classic Blue professional areas are officers, teachers or accountants. Many religiously characterised persons as well as political ones are among them.

4th Level: Blue Group

Just like the Red groups, Blue ones have hierarchies. They are, however, designed differently here. The structure is rather targeted towards large groups that are very strongly structured by distribution of work in a thought-through manner. It is clear who has to perform which responsibilities and tasks. The processes are prescribed in production as well as in communication. There are no special rights of any kind, so that it is particularly easy for members of the group to comply with universal rights and obligations. Several persons share tasks and responsibilities that everyone assumes under his own responsibility. This means that everyone has his own set limits and "tolerances" within which he can make decisions and ensure that all tasks are reliably performed. However, the laws and provisions must be complied with at all times for this. The group members are perfectly honest with each other. It is very important that everything is lawful. The group members live strongly according to their values and principles, which particularly emphasizes their feeling of belonging together.

Status symbols such as consistent equipment of the executive level with offices in solid fine woods or a receptionist are part of presenting this association. Once, I saw how the completely white office furnishing of a department manager at a public-law bank was replaced by brown real-wood furnishings when he was promoted to the outer management circle.

Since the Blue level is not about collecting assets, rewards include things like great company cars, titles or memberships in the local golf club. The military, where obedience is an important value and where no exceptions are tolerated, is also clearly on the Blue level.

4th Level: Blue Organisation

Blue companies have a firm place on markets that have been existing for a while and that offer a certain degree of safety. The focus is not primarily on fast growth, since the company has already developed its fixed position. There is no great competitive pressure, but there are generally different market conditions with which the companies have to deal. They have to position themselves differently to be able to comply with the constantly changing requirements of tomorrow as well. The products produced are complex in general and require high precision and reliability. They are ideal for Blue thinking. Rules in Blue organisations are made to generally be universally applicable and to offer the needed safety. This requires that there are more and more specialists for a department that can meet the requirements in full. For a company on the 4th level, it is important that everything is produced "in-house". This is only possible because it sells a brand that is already established on the market.

Within the organisation, everyone applies the same procedures. Everything that is done is aligned with the rules set up, e.g. in work instructions, user manual and quality standards. It is not always easy for Blue employees to recognise the precise interrelations among the plethora of indices. Documented processes do, however, grant insight to everyone. Nothing is discussed or even implemented in secret. No one in a Blue organisation would ever conceive of acting beyond the borders set for him. In contrast, it would not be expected or even desired either. People like working in their company and enjoy the safety and comfort of not having to "go beyond themselves". They have no reason to look for other employers, which would mean change. They are happy about their usual routine into which their children will grow and enter a position in the company as a matter of course as well. As the miners say: Once a miner, always a miner.

The strategy in Blue companies clearly pursues the objective of securing the company as such and its size. Often, however, there are no clearly defined procedures for developing measures to implement the strategy. Instead, decisions are directly discussed in the management. Including the employees is out of the question.

Company-internal processes are clearly distributed, which may mean that several people are involved in them. Everyone is responsible for one partial area and has to ensure that his tasks in it are performed at the specified quality for the prescribed time. The individual does not care what other areas are doing in this process, since he only focusses on his task and the expectations of his supervisor. The hierarchy is more important to him than the process sequence.

The company shows that the people working in it are important to it by continually raising the wages and salaries. In return, the companies can expect "wages" in the form of loyal employees. However, there may be some problems: In spite of comprehensive support by the IT department, which has an IT system at hand for any function, same areas may have problems with bad integration of these systems. Individual systems being different also do not help a smooth process. These are the classic problems that Blue companies are still fighting with. Former Federal President Köhler once told the Red banks to "return to the virtues of the financier - I deliberately am not using the word banker". He expressed the Blue safety and solidity that was destroyed by Red investment bankers in combination with Orange greed for profit.

A current example for a Blue company is Trigema. Its manager Wolfgang Grupp is particularly proud of never having produced anywhere but in Germany ever since the founding in 1919. The company advertises ecological production, sustainability and secure jobs with its name and has thus reached the age of more than 90 years. With its roughly 1200 employees, Trigema is a classic example for a Blue organisation: large number of employees, guaranteed job safety, clear distribution of work and always foresighted in its products as well as young talent. Nevertheless, the person Wolfgang Grupp surely would have some Purple attributes - or at least that is how he appears in public.

Large traditional administrative organisations with the typical image of a smartly dressed officer behind his polished desk are what we think of on this level. Other Blue organisations are found in many educational centres and in aviation. Before an airline pilot and his co-pilot take the plane onto the runway, they must have shown many Blue virtues and gone through checklists and determined sustainability of the plane. They must observe all provisions. The plane was inspected and serviced at the prescribed intervals. A Red airline wouldn't pay as much attention to that.

5th Level: Orange

This is another level that focusses on its own success. The alignment, however, is not quite as radical as on the Red level, where others often have to suffer from one's own efforts. Orange people will try not to harm others. They always have in mind the ensemble on their way to personal success. Orange persons are clearly target-oriented and often shine with their near-unlimited work effort and increase of performance as a "consequence".

German virtues such as precision, quality, function and longevity are generally deemed secured under the Blue stamp, "Made in Germany". German engineering relies on this as well. Now some companies are trying to engage in Orange cost saving programmes by relocating production into low-wage countries. The seal is then often changed to "Designed in Germany". Not all customers will play along with this or want this to happen. Therefore, some companies have brought back their production already - for example, the bear with the button in his ear.

5th Level: Orange Personal

Career, success, freedom and prosperity are the objectives of people on the Orange level. They want to be the best of their specialisation and thus live good and materially secured. Career is important to them not only because of the money, but also because their performance is more highly recognised in this manner. Their diligence permits them to continually increase their experience. After all, the world is full of opportunities that are only waiting for being taken. They achieve a comfortable degree of independence by their approach. They do not mind technology and science on this path and like to use them in a targeted manner to make life more pleasant and comfortable. With his extreme urging to acquire knowledge and skills, Orange knows when he can rely on himself. He is not adverse to risks. "Nothing ventured, nothing gained" is his principle. Always being up to date is just part of wanting to be right at the top. He is very proud of being a personality with very individual strengths and considers himself to stand above the organisation. This clear I-centricity is classic for the Orange level.

On the 5th level, a person is accordingly self-confident, with strong planning skills and a targeted approach. He usually sees the good things in life and thus skilfully navigates around personal depths. He refuses to let negative thoughts touch him because he knows that they will keep up or even impair his further development. His independence is very important for him. After all, he knows best what he can do and does not need to rely on others to achieve anything.

"Winning" is right at the top of his scale for success. He is certainly able to: Instead of thinking perfectly straight ahead - as is the case on the Blue level - Orange knows that there is a right and a left as well. He perceives the "greater whole" very quickly, sees how things are interrelated and what is happening at the same time, as well as how to deal with things together. This skill of the "all-round look" is a perfect prerequisite for him both as an individual and within a group or organisation. He likes to compete with others to prove his worth to himself and to others. Once he has established a good position for himself, he enjoys the renown he has there. The company for which he works is very important to him. He likes to talk about it. Of course, he only works for companies with a good name on the market. Others wouldn't ever offer him the opportunities he needs for his personal growth. He uses his employer as a medal and valuable reference when he decides to go looking for a new one because the old one no longer offers what he is looking for.

An Orange person therefore is not bound to one company for all his life and would not encourage his children to do so either. This kind of fluctuation makes him a restless companion.

An Orange person with a negative alignment shows strong competitive thinking, performance pressure and greed. Such persons subject themselves to a certain level of stress, which makes them typical candidates for burn-out. They change their ideas very quickly and act aligned with short-term success. Not every outsider will be able to understand the reasons behind their actions at once. Where there is anything to be experienced that is also paying off, he will focus on it in full. Just as interesting work attracts him, fascinating people will, in particular on higher hierarchy levels. If the outer appearance matches his ideas, he will be fascinated to the point where he will gladly ignore a few other "quirks".

The requirement of wanting to get through with things such as change processes too quickly is also typical for negatively characterised Orange persons. All to often employees are forgotten in such an approach. The urge to achieve goals in the short term also falls under this heading which massively endangers a strategic, long-term goal setting. Orange-characterised purchasers often force suppliers down to where quality is no longer guaranteed. Smartphones are an Orange achievement as well as the virtual dependence on them.

An Orange person with a positive alignment has the gift of pulling others along with his positive manner of thinking. Third parties like to see him as an example because his motivation and outstanding performance are just that impressive. Orange persons like to be where there is a lot going on in their working environment: where companies are being restructured, innovative spirit is demanded and things can change quickly, e.g. at Wall Street.

The professional group of investment bankers - or those of them that comply with the rules - are also found on the Orange level. Children love action and have their own objectives (the next Wii game is already in the pipeline), so that holiday jobs will always be taken gladly, even those like weekly mowing of the neighbour's lawn.

5th Level: Orange Group

Groups characterised by Orange demand that each of their members assumes great responsibility. At the same time, they all maintain the characteristic all-round view of everything that is happening in the group, as well as outside of it. Managers can fully rely on their people, which feel that they bear joint responsibility for the group's success and will do anything to support it. Great freedom for decision-making is granted to permit more flexible action. As compared to the Blue group, rules and laws serve a mutual objective, i.e. being able to adjust quickly to changing situations and to act more flexibly.

All in all, rules are limited, however. The company does not want to impair its own progress by measures that are too limiting and would not permit action at the desired speed. Less is better here - after all, the result is to be outstanding. Not only provisions can impair speed, however. Difficult structures take up valuable time as well. Orange groups do not have such structures. Processes that are slowed down will be replaced by more streamline ones that will return the desired speed and flexibility.

Even though every individual in an Orange group wants to be "the best", the group must never be harmed on the way to this objective. Quite the opposite: His effort will benefit everyone else in the community as well. If the entire group profits from his efforts, he can brag that he belongs to it. An individual also does not need to be afraid of others who work well. After all, they also contribute to the group's success, which supports the Orange consciousness of belonging to a successful group. However, it must not reduce his own success.

Competition is an additional incentive on this level, driving members to top performances and additionally motivating them. Premiums or incentives make clear to everyone that the person "honoured" enjoys high recognition, giving him something that he can use to prove his success to third parties as well.

5th Level: Orange Organisation

Orange companies are found in saturated market settings. The emerging buyer´s market demands innovations with shorter and shorter cycles. Companies are under continuous pressure of rising costs. Novelties are continually needed. To specifically warrant the latter for the customers, the focus strongly tends towards core competences and more sophisticated CRM (Customer Relationship Management) – not the least because Orange companies are very interested in binding customers in the long term. Lean management and efficiency increase are applied to keep costs from shooting up into unsustainable heights. The products as such grow more complex, which is controlled at best by the well-organised internal processes. Sales are fit and strong. Administration is perfectly set up and works strategically. Partnerships, e.g. with suppliers, other groups or organisations are going well. This shows how much this attitude towards cooperation differs from those of the 4th level. Those still considered a "simple supplier" are raised to the level of a partner on the 5th level.

Employees in an Orange company will do all they can to make sure that their employer is doing well. Once having managed to get into a company with a established reputation on the market, they are also successful. Orange employees highly identify with their employer and have the customer and market orientation to match. This is good, because every individual is expected to think and act entrepreneurially. No matter the hierarchy level, all people are extremely target-oriented and strive for increased responsibility. In the work processes, a strong sense of duty is delegated as well as action competences. The "view of the greater whole" that is predominant everywhere is also the reason for a very open communication that works wonderfully even beyond the fields.

Since Orange companies always strive to extend their success, they focus on a strategic approach. The employees are included in this manner of work and receive effective tools for implementation to facilitate and accelerate processes.

The hierarchy as such on the Orange level is kept very flat and slim, which also facilitates the overall overview of the company-internal processes. Process areas are distributed among each other and are efficiently and optimally processed. Other processes are also discussed beyond the direct area of responsibility, further improving good interlocking of the areas. The high-quality project organisation and market- and customer-oriented work of every individual in his function makes it possible to dispense with comprehensive administration. This level of the company is much slimmer in Orange enterprises.

New objectives are set for the employees nearly every single year and used as a scale for further personnel development, salary development and possible promotions. Indices that are determined and assessed with IT are used to support these processes. The Balanced Scorecard with its concepts to measure, document and control everything that warrants a smooth process becomes very important.

Another important mark of Orange companies is the consistent win-win strategy. In a business relationship, the partner is seen as equal, so that perfect reconciliation of interest is at the focus for both sides. Profit in the short term is not desired. Long-term, valuable partnerships are the centre of attention.

Companies on the 5th Level mainly focus on their core competences. They tend to be smaller than Blue ones in terms of employee numbers. Specialised service providers that also offer special solutions for sophisticated requirements are found here just as those that offer special products. When a nuclear power plant is suffering problems in Japan, even large parties no longer believe in Orange control of technology and prefer moving towards a change to alternative energies, just as if they had always been against nuclear power. Orange believes in science and technology and feasibility as such. If an event like Fukushima happens in a highly technological country like Japan, the result is different than it was back in Chernobyl, when it was easy to claim that people just weren't able to deal with the situation there. Supporters in France claim that this subject must not be Orangely privatised, but needs to be operated in Blue by the state.

6th Level: Green

Welcome to Woodstock – to use some imagery here. The "flower power" way of thinking of the 6th level clearly shows that this is about community, tolerance and discussion. Woodstock is a "green" event and the Hippie movement was a counter-reaction to Orange. Green was created to better reach objectives together and solve problems by cooperation. Today, Green groups still develop from a wish of better solving the Orange problems. People on this level are cooperative, ready to engage in discussion and less absolute in their arguments and debates than Orange or Blue, which want to convince their conversation partner of the "truth" and win the debate. Green wants to contribute to a mutual solution and will debate nearly without end.

The difference between charity and non-profit organisations makes this clear. Blue non-profits organise correct collections for donations, e.g. at the door, with a booth in front of the super market, or by asking for donations. Green charity events in contrast invite to an event and ask the Orange business people and well-to-dos to come to a gala event with VIPs. The boulevard press is invited as well. Casually speaking, they collect a lot of money quickly with their "Champaign boozing for Uganda". This procedure is unbearable from the point of view of the Blue non-profits, since the costs for this event could have been used to do a whole lot of good. Blue does not see, however, that only this way permits raising a lot of money. Similar discussions have been conducted by the donation consultants at UNICEF.

6th Level: Green Personal

Team building, networking and target achievement: For people on the Green level success has the highest priority as well. However, it is absolutely based on the meeting with other people. Making the right contacts means sustainable personal success for these people. People characterised by Green do not want to improve their own appearance or stand out with special performance, but to bring the right persons together. Relationships are more important to him than the situation. This permits consensus and team spirit but may also lead to endless discussions. He is particularly sensitive for interhuman relationships and places high value on cooperation. Through the permanent communication with his environment, he not only expands his knowledge but can recognise appearing tensions as early as positive developments. Cooperation is very important to him. He is clearly we-centric.

The Green person is very social and knows how to enjoy. He observes, learns, collects experience and continually expands his horizon by reflexion and exchange. His strong consciousness makes him very well able to "listen inside himself." His intuition will tell him if he is thinking into the right direction. He is capable of reading "between the lines". This form of sensitivity makes him a perfect group person. His social competences are as helpful in the project team as in the work with the customer, including admitting emotions as well as honesty and valuation of others, turning him into a highly valued conversation partner and team colleague. If he needs to make decisions, he will listen to all sides first and then balance his opinion. He is often the pole of stability who keeps an overview of the entire thing and acts as a mediator, in particular in volatile matters. This ability helps him and gives him personal confirmation. At the same time, this is what makes him emotionally strongly dependent on the group. Equality of both sexes is as important to him as equal opportunities, fairness, empathy and cooperation. Continuous exchange with others is particularly important to him. He perceives it as a personal gain.

A person characterised by Green is open to the world and has a high sense of responsibility towards others. He would never trigger anything that may be a disadvantage for others or even harm them. The most positive thing about him is his skill of performing actual teamwork.

Of course, this level also has a negative alignment of consciousness, which makes the persons affected thus unable to make decisions. They will discuss a lot without ever coming to conclusion - let alone doing anything about it. A very strong emotional orientation supports this as well. The negatively characterised Green person also runs at risk of losing sight of reality and suddenly acting only for the purpose instead of cooperatively. All in all, persons with a Green consciousness tend to be found in multifunctional teams.

6th Level: Green Group

The Green group is characterised by its heterogeneous make-up that permits everyone in it to use the skills and qualifications of the others in the best fashion possible. Cooperation within the group is characterised by tolerance, mutual valuation and acceptance. Conflicts appear rather rarely since harmony plays an important role. If there are any disputes at some point, everyone involved will be heard before a conclusion is finally reached. As already mentioned in the beginning, this level is in a way a counter reaction to Orange, which is mainly performance- and profit-oriented. Green in contrast returns to human values. When success becomes apparent, it is not considered a short-term achievement from the here and now but the result of the right cooperation with the right kind of team. This strengthens team spirit and association, which is considered absolutely pleasant. The differences of the group members are even supported further to receive the largest scope of skills in one pool.

In a Green group, there is nearly no hierarchy. In rare cases, there is one with two levels. Each individual in the group is a personality that is equally responsible for the functioning. Every group member is therefore taken seriously and accepted and his work is highly valued and considered an important part of the whole. Newcomers are always welcome, are quickly integrated and enrich the group by their special qualifications. The mutual forces are similar to those on the levels Purple and Blue, but external persons may also profit by the achievements of the Green group. When the team works perfectly towards the outside, it is no problem if an individual in it steps back a little, as long as general good does not suffer under it. Sometimes this can even make the team as a whole more successful. This shows true understanding of a team! Cohesion is also supported by mutual activities.

As always, there are also negative characteristics here, specifically if the Green person has a stronger need to be accepted and to belong under all circumstances. He tends to overestimate his strengths because he wants to provide special benefit for the group under all circumstances. He will quickly overtax himself. The danger of burn-out is particularly high in negatively characterised Green people.

Green groups are often found in social areas, everywhere in connection with, e.g., environmental and climate protection, and in independent church groups that are also socially dedicated.

6th Level: Green Organisation

The market on which the 6th level is found is an absolute demand market. The products found and needed there are high-quality and innovative prod-

ucts that are "rare to find". The wide qualification range of Green is perfect for niche areas and also known for unusual products that offer added value to the customer. The number of employees in Green companies is rather low, but the turnover can easily be compared even to large groups. It becomes clear that lots of work therefore is performed by external companies. After all, they will just as gladly get support from the outside as they focus on internal specialists that permit turnover at a higher scope. These specialists are very highly valued.

The employees are continually motivated and consider themselves valuable members of their community according to the motto of "We are strong together and will reach our objectives for the good of all!" They are subject to a continuous incentive that shows every single person the sense of his actions. Everyone knows that his core competences are important for this community and its success and likes to put them to use. Very different skills are deliberately combined and many organisations find benefits in this for their positioning on the market. Wherever many different personalities meet, errors will happen, of course. They are, however, not perceived as obstacles or even punished, but actively used for mutual further development. Questions are asked about why these errors have occurred to better understand their causes and counter them accordingly.

Looking at this strategy, it is very much reminiscent to that of the Orange level with focus on success, customer commitment, sustainability, etc. However, on the Green level, man as a valued individual is at the centre of things with all of his skills and core competences. Everything that is being done is striven for the good of the employees, both in the present and for the future.

Tasks and functions are not mapped in hierarchies but in a matrix structure that is to warrant a high coordination of all functions and line jobs. To ensure this, there are multiple reporting paths among each other and teams that work complementarily and multifunctionally. These project teams are reassembled according to demand and requirements. There are also often true project organisations within the teams, which contribute to decision-making, role and task distribution.

The processes as such are all "sophisticated", also because everyone does his best to make them work. If something in the process is not working quite right, newer, better-fitting competences are brought in to continue to warrant a smooth procedure. The governance processes regarding employee management and to secure mutual corporate objectives are just as sophisticated.

The tools from the Orange level that are needed for success are maintained and supplemented by team premiums. The technical possibilities of support are also used, more often, in particular regarding communication and cooperation. Of course, the performance rendered is compensated accordingly, with the salary system being as consistent as possible and kept transparently for everyone. Working time is not clocked as strictly, but no one must incur any kind of disadvantage from this.

People on the Green level are particularly characterised by accepting that all people are different. This skill makes them particularly cooperative partners who are also able to keep themselves back if the situation requires.

Wherever innovation is needed - e.g. in the automotive industry - Green groups can be found. This also includes service companies that have specialised in a niche area and can make use of their special know-how.

The First and the Second Tier

The levels you have gotten to know up to now are subject to the term "Level of the first tier". This means that all people on this level react to needs that occur in their own living environment. They are "caught" in their view of things and cannot see more than one perspective. This skill is only developed with the second tier. From here onwards, the levels repeat, focussing now on sense and meaning. This is the decisive component that is added on this higher rank: Sense and relevance of the previous levels are recognised and complexity noticeably increases.

7th Level: Yellow

The levels you have learned about up to now have viewed each other without understanding for the others and classified the "goings-on" in the other colours as tending to be wrong. This will change now! This is where we set out into a new dimension - and suddenly, the importance of the other levels is valued as well. Yellow sees everything from several perspectives as "yearns" for knowledge. Exciting subjects are quickly focussed on and just as quickly let go again when they turn boring and routine. Professor Graves made an interesting test with his students. He classified them by main level and first gave them the order of finding a group speaker. The Blues took the oldest, the Orange the one with the best performance, the Green discussed it and the Yellows asked what was going to come next, as they wanted to determine their group speaker anew for every task and replace him as required, even during the task.

Many start-ups, in particular during the Internet euphoria in the late 1990s, were founded by Yellows who went self-employed with innovative ideas and managed to acquire money from Orange holding companies. Many start-ups with Yellow founders were unable to expand because they were missing Blue structures and organisation, Orange sales power and Green willingness to talk. Many founders also left the companies again quickly when things became less exciting. This is a typical Yellow vice.

7th Level: Yellow Personal

 Even though multi-perceptiveness is focussed on here, persons on the 7th level have clear patterns for their thought and action. Not only do they see the benefits of the previous levels, but also know how to use and combine them. Their systematic and strategic thinking becomes more abstract and offers many ideas and concepts to find clear paths to the objective.

They use their comprehensive competence and networking to get to the intended targets in all areas important for them. Growth and further development must be vivid and should take place continually. Change is always welcome, since it offers the diversity Yellows need. They are limited to what is most logical and necessary to act pragmatically and responsibly. They like to use systems that support them in their projects. Being independent, acquiring lots of knowledge, being creative and acting independently is of outstanding importance to them. In contrast to Green, Yellow persons have no problem handling ambiguous statements or situations. They do not need to discuss them until everyone comes to an agreement, like people from the previous levels. Quite the opposite: They accept different opinions next to each other, a concept that would perfectly confuse the "Green". This also applies to paradox thinking and principles that contradict each other, but are no problem for people on the 7th level. They see this rather as an incentive for expanding their knowledge. This knowledge turns them into people with a high self-estimation who can easily admit that they do not know something. After all, they can consider this again elsewhere and use it for their own good. The knowledge they have already gained and the ability of taking up and accepting feelings are also built on this strong self-confidence.

The "Yellow" person learns without cease, according to his own ideas and uses all the resources that are offered. He loves experiments and can deal with taking a fall from time to time. Such new experiences only additionally expand their horizon. Their thirst for knowledge makes them particularly sensitive with a great talent for recognising and interpreting emotions. This "expand me" turns them into true masters of learning who also like to be alone to intensify their experience of themselves. They strive for personal further development more strongly than wishing to become prosperous and powerful. If a person characterised by Yellow meets a person from any other level, he will find it easy to meet this person on "eye level" and adjust to him at least for the moment of the meeting for the sake of communication. A Yellow person considers every level important and indispensable for the overall system. He lives and acts freely according to his personal motto of: "A world of black and white is boring - only many shades make it interesting." He knows that everyone can move up or down on the colourful stairway, depending on his personal value system.

He always wants to know what others are thinking, but only because the ideas of others can support him in making his own decisions. He is not dependent on this, however. He is merely curious. In a relationship, the Yellow person highly values his partner and has no wish to possess him or her. Compared to persons of the Red and Orange levels, he appropriately focusses on the individual. He remains himself even when he meets with people of other levels on "eye level". This authenticity turns him into a valued conversation partner who always meets others openly. Personal development being of the utmost importance for him turns him into an I-centric person.

Often, the person characterised by Yellow appears arrogant, cold and distant because of this egocentricity. Negative characteristics are accordingly condescending-seeming impatience, "isolating oneself", being insensitive to the feelings of others, which may even lead to the "Yellow" being perceived as ruthless and egotistic. They also tend to overestimate themselves.

Positively characterised Yellow persons are open and tolerant towards third parties and their needs. They are extremely flexible and do not "insist" on the persistence of things. What fits and works well today may be out-dated tomorrow. However, they also see that a certain persistence applies for some things that will remain the same beyond tomorrow: in behavioural, mental and emotional aspects alike. Vice versa, things considered wrong once may still be wrong later.

7th Level: Yellow Group

The Yellow group engages in intense networking, which requires high flexibility. The things that groups, systems or individuals of the other levels offer, with all of their core competences, is not only very interesting for Yellow, but also of great benefit for his own further development. Yellows use their communication skills for this as well as their creativity, which makes them interesting to others as well if they are open-minded for this. If there is any dispute, it will be discussed openly and dealt with within the group. This works well because everyone will pass on information without concealing or hiding anything. Fixed structures within the group as they were maintained by the previous levels increasingly lose in importance. Instead, hierarchical and non-hierarchical structures of very different learning and working methods are included. The Yellow group now starts to include working models of other levels into their work for a while. This would be unthinkable for any groups from the previous levels! The reason for this new skill is in the flexibility of Yellow: Structures, processes and rules of other levels are combined with each other to reach the objective in the best manner possible. Since the Yellow group is acting in loose networks, it can only be controlled through clear target specifications and rules defined in advance. Its objectives are either set directly by the Yellow group, depending on how it is made up, or for it. The things needed are organised. Once the target has been defined, the group assembles from individuals and partially other groups so that the objective can be reached best.

Continuous learning, increase of knowledge and further development is of the utmost importance for the Yellow group. It particularly strives to be independent and absolutely open towards the other group members. Of course, there are hierarchies as well, but they are not permanent and can be completely restructured again when the next task is set. The experiment Professor Graves did with his students showed this very nicely. The group members know that they need each other and their mutual know-how to reach their goals. It is enough to know what the others can do and where his weaknesses are to find the best combination for a task. Everything the members of the previous levels fear or have to do become less and less important here. This way, Yellow renders better results and ideas and delivers higher quality and quantity.

There are not very many examples for Yellow groups, since these groups keep reassembling at need. If a Blue state employs Yellow hackers to fight Red organised crime, or groups of thinkers meet to feed the "free encyclopaedia" Wikipedia, Yellow people are (virtually) meeting for a purpose. We have to thank the Internet and its possibilities for this!

7th Level: Yellow Organisation

Just like the market for Green, the market for Yellow companies is a market of demand. However, it has an even higher claim: The best quality and most innovative thing is demanded. Yellow is perfectly set up for offering this. Because it wants to continually reassemble as needed, Yellow is always able to make use of the very best that is needed for the respective demand. With the far-reaching network, other companies and their competences can be "tapped" once their core competences are in demand. This is not considered a disadvantage by the network partners, but supported because they proceed among each other in the same manner. Green organisations, which are also acting on niche markets, would be helpless with this approach, which makes Yellow the perfect pro in matters of innovation. For the Yellow organisation, it is important to be able to integrate oneself. Every single individual is open towards the others and provides the basis for partnership and cooperation. Everyone knows that he is able to use his knowledge effectively and always strives to contribute his know-how in the best fashion possible. It is very nearly the best motivation possible at all! Independent action is just as important as responsibility for it. The continuous exchange of knowledge serves to expand the personal horizon that permits every individual to be particularly creative for optimising things in communication or work processes.

The product or service on the Yellow level is above the company as such. Just as on the Green level, sustainability is emphasised here.

The Yellow organisation makes the impossible possible: For example, Orange salesmen and Blue quality assurance are "combined" with brave Red designers to implement a special customer demand. The strong networking skills make projects process as smoothly as none of the previous levels could.

Processes are very sophisticated and continually developed further and optimised. In this manner, they can be quickly adjusted to changing underlying situations.

IT is mandatory for this level, since a great part of the work is happening on a virtual level. Systems that support cooperation, communication and expansion of knowledge are used predominantly. This type of work creates lots of freedom for the individual and offers working times that are perfectly flexible. Everyone can devise from where or how or when he works. The only thing important is that they responsibly contribute.

8th Level: Turquoise

On this level, we remain in the second tier, i.e. we retain the skill of understanding the sense and relevance of the previous levels and see them in a different degree of complexity. As compared with the first tier, this level can be seen as the "Turquoise-Purple". All action and work is aligned with sustainability, holistic approaches and the well-being of the world. There is lots of idealism arising on this level, since the knowledge of Yellow and the faith in the swarm intelligence of the global interrelations, as well as the wish of "saving the world" are combined. Turquoise believes that it is perfectly possible to create a lifestyle that can be used by any being and fully focuses on well-being for the entire world. With its selflessness, it not only observes but is able to design. As compared to the first tier, Turquoise is the Purple of the second tier.

8th Level: Turquoise Personal

This level is about the whole and retention of what has been achieved. People here have high ideals, a strong spiritual consciousness and a comprehensive view of the things in the world. These characteristics make it possible for them to often impress others with their extraordinary ideas and to interpret things perfectly in a different way. In all they do, they fully trust their instincts and intuition, and demand that their actions be sustainable. Turquoise tries to solve the unsolved problems of Yellow and thus has a greater responsibility for the community and everything around it. He is we-centric. He knows that everything he does has consequences and painstakingly considers his own decisions. Turquoise is very present in discussions and, like Yellow, will move to the conversation partner's level. He is easily able to imagine himself in his shoes. What he says is clear to everyone at once, which makes him more pleasant for his partner in conversations.

Turquoise uses the knowledge of all previous levels for the general good on this level. People here have a very sharp perception and walk through the world with the greatest perceptive faculty of all. They can mentally and spiritually open so far that they recognise possibilities and ways just as errors and misperceptions, which is something that the persons on other levels have never been able to do. Their limitations, rules, forces and doctrines did not permit them access to this. In spite of these outstanding skills, however, Turquoise is not better or happier. Again, there are negative alignments that are expressed in native or radical action or that show proof of virtually unlimited idealism.

8th Level: Turquoise Group

Networking is brought to previously unseen perfection on this level. A Turquoise group is able to keep together many different levels, to recognise things that harmoniously interact, integrate groups and individuals and combine attitude as well as science. This gives birth to something new that focuses on the world as a whole and assesses everything according to this holon not being injured. The group considers itself to be a truly holistic team without competition, without man-made rules and the connected wish for long-term overall use for all.

8th Level: Turquoise Organisation

Companies on this level are virtually non-existent at this time. Companies with a Turquoise touch are committed to high ethical values and align their actions with them. Interestingly, many spiritual and integral fighters are rather Blue debaters with a Turquoise shading. The Orange business world very sceptically and confusedly looks at these groups and appearances. Terms such as "Corporate Social Responsibility" have generally resulted from the Turquoise area but are often used in an

Orange manner. Of course, many companies hope to make social and cultural commitment usable in marketing technology as well. Therefore, the "go green" campaigns of companies always also require questioning the motivation and original thought.

I have not found any Turquoise organisations yet. Even amnesty international, WWF or Greenpeace are not on this level as organisations. The time for Turquoise organisations will come though.

9th Level: Coral

Coral is the Red of the second tier. People on this level know that all limits are generated by human action and being. In his egocentricity, man here is not solely striving for power and renown without concern for the collateral damage, but shows a high respect towards all life forms. People in his environment will feel motivated and supported. They will grow beyond their previous limits and discover new things.

THE TRANSFERS BETWEEN THE LEVELS

What makes people leave a level and how are their value systems designed? This is an important question that you are right to ask.

When do these triggers and transfers to the next higher level happen?

> » In the 1st level (Beige), when people get the impression that their existence is dependent on a mysterious and partially scary world, they will look for protection and explanation together with others. They will cooperate to interpret and understand the world. They have solved the problems of the first level and are able to secure their existence in the here and now.

> » In the 2nd level (Purple), when the feeling occurs that one is able to achieve more on one's own by leaving the protection of the community and going through with "one's own thing". People leave the fetters or tribe or family (the training company) to become independent.

> » In the 3rd level (Red), when a kind of conscience is developed. Feelings of guilt appear and people start looking for a meaningful cooperation and order, as well as to create rules.

> » In the 4th Level (Blue), when there is self-awakening and one strives for freedom. People want to try out their own skills, set their own objectives and reach them out of their own power. Authorities are questioned and freedoms are tested.

» In the 5th Level (Orange), when the wish for greater cooperation in a social system arises that strives for acceptance and belonging to find inner harmony but also to achieve targets together.

» In the 6th Level (Green), when there is inquisitive self-awakening and one strives for mutual dependence that is free of a need for applause and recognition but would gladly and well cooperate with others at need.

» In the 7th Level (Yellow), when the wish increases to combine this knowledge in new paths to recover the natural balance and harmony of earth.

RESISTANCE TO VALUE SYSTEMS

In addition to belonging to a value level, however, people may also dislike and resist a value level - or its specific value characteristics.

Resistance to levels

In order to better illustrate the measurements of the resistances, we would first like to show what is meant by a resistance in the sense of the 9 Levels of Value Systems Theory. Examples in the following illustrate with the help of levels what the resistances are directed against.

Resistance in general and in terms of the 9 Levels of Value Systems

Resistance can be understood as a counter-effect experienced by a will, an action, a force or a movement through another. In a management-oriented sense, resistance is understood as a negative reaction to changes, e.g. in structures, processes or entire systems. Resistance occurs in particular when the breaking up of proven structures or process flows encounters negative behaviour on the part of individual employees. Those affected by this experience changes as emotional turmoil and initially regard them as unpleasant and lacking freedom, with the aim of restoring their own freedom of action. The intensity of resistance depends, among other things, on how important the affected person sees the restriction and how intensively he is prepared to offer resistance.

Likewise, resistance can also be seen as a protective function that individuals, teams and organizations develop to protect themselves from excessive demands and supposedly absurd or harmful changes. Within the framework of a change process, however, resistance can also be desirable, since those involved signal interest and concern. It also serves as a source of information for managers, because it helps them to understand the needs of their employees.

Steering resistors into productive paths

One of the main tasks in the change process is to integrate resistance into the change process through suitable measures. In this way, resistance is to be directed into the productive path of individuals, departments or the entire company and suitable techniques for conflict resolution are to be used.

The 9 Levels of Value Systems focuses on resistance directed towards value systems. If someone has resistance to value systems or value levels, this is made clear by the fact that the person does not agree with the values and the ways of thinking and behaving derived from them. The opposite is the case: there is a backlash. Depending on your preferred level of values, this can have different dimensions and intensities. In this context, Graves refers to the active or passive rejection of value levels.

Resistances in the levels

Each level can also create resistance, which can have different reasons. On the one hand, it is possible that the person affected has a low level and is therefore unfamiliar with these value systems. On the other hand, the person may have had negative experiences with this value system, so that resistance has arisen. It is also possible that the value systems are contrary to one's own value systems.

Examples:

If a person has the main characteristic green and prefers cooperative and consensus-oriented arrangements, a red value system, which prefers fast and situative decisions, can cause resistance (in doubt without arrangement).

If the main characteristic is purple and rituals and traditions are adhered to, this often creates resistance with orange, because from their point of view these people are brakes on progress and growth.

This opposite effect often occurs when levels are opposite each other and have two levels in between, e.g. Purple/Orange, Red/Green or Blue/Yellow.

Anyone who is aware of their own value systems as a person, group or organisation also knows at the same time against which level rejections and/or resistance exist. The measurement of these resistances is important because this is exactly where the problems arise in everyday life. People do not feel well, tensions arise in groups and conflicts arise in organisations.

Four possibilities for combining resistors with the value systems

Basically there are four classical possibilities in the interaction of the value systems and the resistances on the same level.

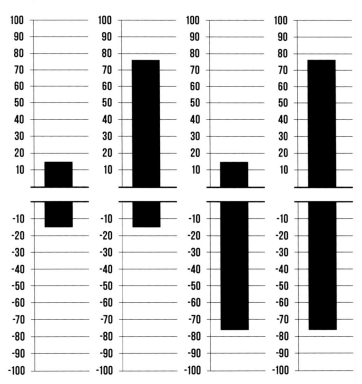

Small level and small resistance

In this combination the value system is not very pronounced, and at the same time there is no resistance to it. For example, for a blue level, this could mean that the blue is not pronounced, but the person has no problems with it. In casual terms, the person might be happy if everything is well organised.

High level and low resistance

In this combination, the values of this level are highly pronounced and thus guiding for action. At the same time, there is no resistance within or against this level. An example of this is purple: the purple man is strongly attached to his homeland, loves rituals and cohesion over long periods. At the same time, there is no resistance if someone is travelling with similar value systems and elements.

Small level and big resistance

Here the value system is not very pronounced and at the same time the person disturbs the value system. An example of this is orange. In these people, orange (dynamics, goal orientation, proactivity, etc.) is not very pronounced, but at the same time it disturbs when it comes into contact with these values.

Great level and great resistance

In this constellation one also speaks of an ambivalence. A value system is very pronounced, but at the same time you also experience a rejection of this level. An example of this is a strong red colour: The person here prefers values such as dominance, strength, power and impulsive assertiveness - but at the same time is in resistance when another person with the same values approaches him or he is possibly even more dominant and powerful than he himself. Another example is a high green character with a lot of harmony and involvement, as well as consensus orientation.

Examples from everyday life

The Head of Department

A department head of a patriarchically run company has a very high cooperative and consensus-oriented management attitude, which is also reflected in the high green. He has massive problems when appearing in his department or from outside the red department, which even causes him health problems. Its high green and its low red make it difficult for it to survive against the red. He interpreted the high resistance in purple as follows: "It bothers me if employees stick to traditional procedures or if employees feel protected just because their father is division manager.

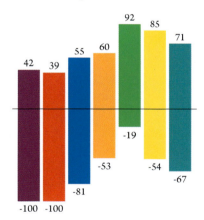

The creative, free-thinking coach

Our coach is a creative lady who works as a sparring partner, is very free-spirited and reluctant to work on administrative and business-oriented projects. If she comes into contact with projects that require a lot of small stuff and structured administrative work, she can carry them out, but with reluctance. If something is looking for too strong processes or profit maximization, she finds this disturbing.

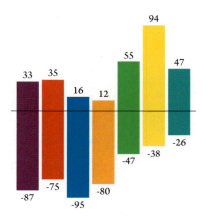

Expat who no longer wants to go to corporate headquarters

Our IT expert and head of department, who returns after 5 years of work abroad, can no longer imagine returning to the German corporate headquarters. He feels trapped in these rather rigid constructs, some of which are corruptly infiltrated, so that he does not want to return there under any circumstances.

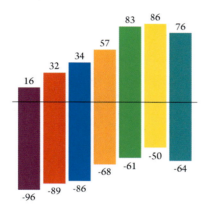

CHANGE MANAGEMENT IN THE MODEL

The Phases of Change

Between the feeling of being on the perfectly right level to the actual change, people go through different phases that I will briefly describe below:

Stability
The system (company, department) feels comfortable and can deal with the challenges of the environment. There is no need for change yet.

Unrest
The first interferences occur. People start to deal with the changing environment. Reasons for destabilisation may be changed market situations, changed customer structures, changed competence pressure, as well as new competitors, new products, new methods, new technologies. It is also possible that destabilisation results from changes of the company itself. The company has grown a lot - organically or by merger. The company has entered new markets or has a new management. The reasons are manifold, but all lead to unrest.

Crisis
Today, however, the impulse for changes is rarely given by the understanding that pervasive change is required. The actual change happens under great pressure, due to crises of partially great scope.

Movement
A phase of euphoria follows. People start to euphorically design the change. The change is actively implemented. In the phase of move-

ment, the management has to ensure that the planned actions will not turn into actionism. The target must not be forgotten. Employees must not suddenly run out of breath in the middle of the change process either. Often, old habits are taken up again then and the change fails. Only when the change has been completed, can rest and safety return to the company. A new condition of stability has resulted.

Change Stages

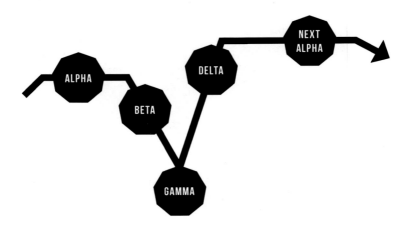

ALPHA	Phase of stability and congruence. Solutions and problems fit together.
BETA	Time of insecurity and doubt, as some problems cannot be solved, but it is not sure why this is the case.
GAMMA	State of fear/worry and frustration, because problems/challenges seem unsolvable.
DELTA	A breakthrough of new thinking seems to be reached in order to solve the so far unsuperable problems.
NEXT ALPHA	The complexity of the problem and the way of dealing with it are internalised, so that new stability arises.
NEXT BETA	New doubt and sorrows emerge. New, more complex issues are detected.

Prerequisites for changes

Before starting a change process – before either developing further within the level or even leaving it to move onto the next – two important things must be clarified: Is the person able of going through this personal change (does he have the skills and abilities as well as the know-how required for the change) and does he even want to take this step (is he really ready for it, "ripe" and motivated)?

COMPETENCE	WILLINGNESS
1. **Potential for change** (skills and proficiencies, being substantially prepared). 2. **Sovereign solutions** for the actual level of the 9 levels. 3. **Appropriate dealing** with obstacles that occur. 4. **Integration of the learnings,** consolidation of change and support in the change process.	5. **Openness** for the necessity of changes and a change process. 6. **Dissonance,** discomfort in the current level of the 9 levels resp. in the current situation. 7. **Insight** in the benefits of change, the utility that can be obtained by change.

[Translated from source: Cf. Bär-Sieber/Krumm/Wiehle: Unternehmen verstehen, gestalten, verändern – das Graves-Value-System in der Praxis, Wiesbaden, 2015]

Direction of Changes in the Model

Changes are not always performed from one level to the other - changes are possible within a level as well. This is actually rather frequently the case. Where a person finally moves to depends on the environmental conditions that initiate the necessity of change.

On One Level

Changing within one level happens often. Present processes and mechanisms are stabilised or recovered. Light corrections within a level are possible as well.

Up

A change upwards always means complete re-orientation. This means a change from WE- to I-centricity or vice versa. Levels cannot be skipped. The system has no elevator!

Down

A change downwards usually means regression. A system may face severe problems and not manage to move or develop to the next higher level. Therefore, the company returns to old "recipes and virtues" of a level below.

THE 9 LEVELS IN PRACTICE

The world, society and economy are subject to continuous change. Companies have to be able to develop and adjust to new situations if they want to continue to be competitive on the market. CEO studies prove what is mainly known:

» 79% of the directors say that complexity clearly increases.
» 92% say that change management is important.
» 78% declare that ability to change is important.
» 94% consider corporate culture important for success.

The value commission also writes in its executive survey that quality of value systems is more strongly at the focus in times of economic uncertainty and large macroeconomic unrest. Companies that consider their business on clearly defined value systems sustainably and in the long term will be able to deal with such strong changes on the market much better. If innovation cycles turn shorter, marketing strategies more risky, corporate funding subject to higher prerequisites and the presence of "soft" productivity benefits such as motivation and ability to perform are decisive, the value system of company, management and staff increasingly makes the difference in competition.

The survey of the value commission about the contribution of values to corporate success shows a clear result as well: More than 90 % of the executives estimate this amount to be "very high" or "high".

Markets change, customer needs and requirements are no longer the same, new generations are looking for different working conditions and job models. Technical advances and changed political framework conditions ensure that employees, departments and companies have to adjust.

How should the company change, though?

Many directors and managers are subject to continuous pressure to improve the company and its culture because the former success has disappeared. Additionally, the company is unable to deal with the changed conditions. New problems usually cannot be solved with old solutions. There are simple reasons for this: Employees and processes are aligned with what has been tried and tested. The decision-makers are often lacking starting points.

They want a measurable and tangible instrument that can be used for management and employees alike.

Organisation development pioneer Prof. Edgar Schein defines corporate culture as follows: "A pattern of shared basic assumptions that the group learned as it solved its problems of external adaptation and internal integration." This assumption presented by him is based on the value systems in groups and organisations.

With the Model of 9 Levels of Value Systems, value systems of persons, groups and organisations can be measured and a special consciousness can be created for them. It shows where the levers for change are located while also making clear how important changes may be. The often rather unspecific feeling of "needing to change" is made more tangible. With a central model and the three perspectives of person, group and organisation, we can work on specific subjects individually and in a customised manner with a single consistent model, which makes handling much easier.

The Model of 9 Levels has two sides that are facing each other like a kind of pendulum movement, comparable to a spiral staircase: During dynamic development, a person, group or organisation always moves back and forth from WE- to I-centricity. There is no elevator in this spiral staircase model. Levels cannot be skipped.

Dynamics and further development of one's own value systems is always at the centre. So is the question of how these value systems are going to match the current challenge in our own lives. This is particularly important and differs from other static models that have to be continually adjusted to new situations in its manner of thinking. In the model of 9 Levels, stations of development of persons, groups and organisations can accordingly be reflected on and assessed regarding changes to the environment, market and competition.

Typical levers for change are

- » Mission / vision / value
- » Strategy
- » Leadership
- » Qualification
- » Target systems
- » Structures
- » Processes / tasks

The persons responsible often try to change the behaviour. However, this is rarely sustainable and will often not be pervasive enough because people are not sufficiently conscious of the necessity of change. If pervasive changes are to be implemented in companies, departments and persons, they must be targeted at the value systems. The above levers for change must be reconciled with the desired value system. Often, changes may be desired but the target systems remain the old ones. This cannot work! If more exchange, cooperation and best practice is desired, the compensation system or key-performance indicators must not facilitate direct competition.

Generally, persons, groups and organisations can be more successful and better handle the challenges of the living environment, if their value systems match the current challenges– i.e. if they are reconciled. If the living conditions in the central elements are Orange – targeted, powerful and career-oriented - people, groups and organisations with a high Orange share in their value systems will be much more successful than Blue systems which prefer to act according to rules, loyalty and order. This is not about "the higher the better", but about what fits well. If the value system of a company is Green but the market and competition are Red, problems will arise.

Looking at the German-speaking countries, most companies are mainly facing challenges for developing from Blue to Orange or from Orange to Green.

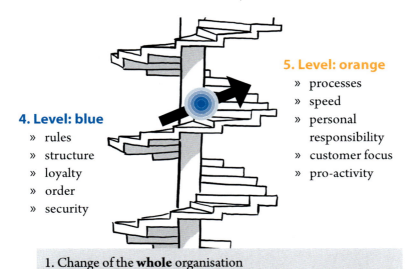

4. Level: blue

» rules
» structure
» loyalty
» order
» security

5. Level: orange

» processes
» speed
» personal
  responsibility
» customer focus
» pro-activity

1. Change of the **whole** organisation
2. **Competence** (capability to change)
3. **Willingness** (readiness for change)
4. Change as a specifically developed and consistent **process**

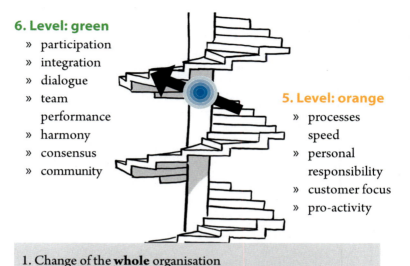

6. Level: green

- » participation
- » integration
- » dialogue
- » team performance
- » harmony
- » consensus
- » community

5. Level: orange

- » processes speed
- » personal responsibility
- » customer focus
- » pro-activity

1. Change of the **whole** organisation
2. **Competence** (capability to change)
3. **Willingness** (readiness for change)
4. Change as a specifically developed and consistent **process**

We are ready for new solutions. Many people, decision-makers and companies are facing complex and novel challenges and problems and have experienced that established concepts are no longer working. The model of 9 Levels now provides a proven and internationally tested model that breaks down the complexity in a scientifically founded manner and summarises the subject into a pragmatic model.

I wish you great success.

Yours, Rainer Krumm

CULTURAL CHANGE – CASE

Starting position

A medium-sized mechanical engineering company had hardly changed for many years. Due to changes in the market (increasing competition, high cost pressure, shorter delivery time expectations, etc.) it was more and more forced to work more dynamically and faster, which has hardly been possible so far.

The newly formed change team now started the cultural change with external support. It was important for the team to be able to measure the change in order to better grasp and control the soft factors.

Way of proceeding

The graphic below gives an overview of the different phases of the change process.

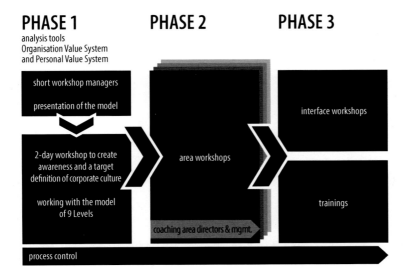

PHASE 1
analysis tools
Organisation Value System
and Personal Value System

short workshop managers

presentation of the model

2-day workshop to create awareness and a target definition of corporate culture

working with the model of 9 Levels

PHASE 2

area workshops

coaching area directors & mgmt.

PHASE 3

interface workshops

trainings

process control

Phase 1

In a 2-hour short workshop the 9 levels model was presented and together with the change team an analysis of the current challenges was worked out. This consisted of two managing directors, the personnel manager and the sales manager.

The change team was convinced of the sense of purpose and thus set the further process in motion. After the short workshop, the entire change team completed both a Personal Value System (PVS) and an Organisation Value System (OVS).

This was followed by a 2-day workshop for this change team, in which the model was discussed in more detail. The results of the 9 level surveys and their significance for the people and especially the organisation were discussed in detail and concrete steps and target definitions were defined.

Agenda of the workshop:

- » Typical! Just like us!
- » Why is corporate culture so important and how can it be changed?
- » Value systems of individuals, groups and organisations
- » The model of the 9 levels: making value systems measurable
- » The own company in model and in reality
- » Your own Personal Value System: self-reflection
- » Case studies and examples from other companies
- » What does your company have to do in order to master the challenges?
- » The role of leadership in corporate culture
- » How do systems, organization and processes fit into the necessary corporate culture
- » Understanding and regarding change as a path

» Deriving measures and steps
» Outlook for the next concrete steps

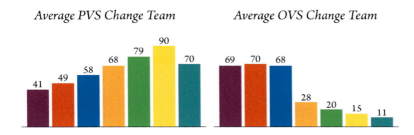

Average PVS Change Team   *Average OVS Change Team*

The change team developed the ORANGE target vision and, as an intermediate stage of the change process, stabilization in BLUE to limit the RED.

Phase 2

Two further workshops were held, each of which took one day. The Personal Value System and the Organisation Value System were used to record the value systems over 9 levels in advance.

On the one hand, with the division heads, whereby the change team was also present in order to strengthen communication and create a common basis for the change.

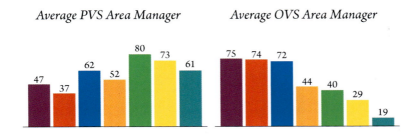

Average PVS Area Manager   *Average OVS Area Manager*

On the other hand, with the works council. The early involvement of the works council proved itself, so that it could also be integrated as a supporter of the change process. This had a high symbolic value in the commercial sector. Here, at the end of the workshop, the change team was added to discuss the results and goal definitions together. The results of the 9 levels survey were now presented to each other and their significance for the organisation were discussed.

Average PVS Works Council   *Average OVS Works Council*

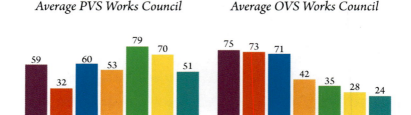

It is particularly interesting to note that the individuals in all groups were much more advanced in their development than the organisation itself. So why had it not (yet) succeeded in moving them in the desired direction?

The graphic representation of the value systems and the understanding of their significance for the company enables a new view of the situation and provides a solid basis for diverse discussions and the development of further steps.

Phase 3

From the various ACTUAL analyses, the TARGET is worked out together. Concrete steps and training and workshop topics were:

- » Workshop: Clarify conflicts of objectives between the departments
- » Management training for all levels: Creation of a uniform understanding of management
- » Leadership workshop "Impact"
- » Individual coaching of managers
- » Introduction of performance-based salary systems
- » Office layout: Design of communication-promoting office structures
- » Communication workshop on the topic of change
- » Lean management in production and administration

While the purple and blue levels should continue to ensure stability, order and quality assurance, everyone involved wishes for a further change from red to blue and a long-term development towards orange.

Result after the 1-year change process

After about a year, another OVS survey of the change team, the works council and the division heads took place in order to reflect the positive impression of the managers through 9 levels. The results were as follows:

BEFORE: **AFTER:**

Average OVS Change Team

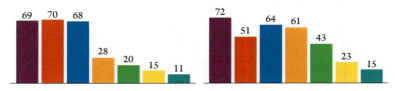

Average OVS Area Manager

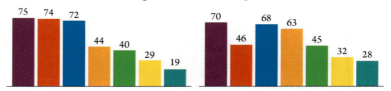

Average OVS Works Council

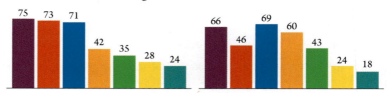

The cultural change with the support of the 9 levels has obviously succeeded. The importance of tradition and local roots was retained. The characteristics on the blue level are also almost unchanged, which remained stable. The desire to reduce the red portion was also implemented. A movement towards orange and the first steps towards green have already become apparent.

AREAS OF APPLICATION

Cultural change

Situation & needs

Many companies like to cling to the old ways – after all, things that worked in the past will surely work in the future. The result is that for several years, these companies will undergo little or no change. However, market conditions have likely undergone considerable change: increasing competition, rising costs, and higher delivery expectations force companies to work more quickly and dynamically – but this is virtually impossible to implement. A cultural change needs to take place in order to make this company competitive again. A task that can usually not be implemented without external technical assistance.

Why 9 Levels?

Cultural change is often accompanied by complex processes, which need to be made accessible to all employees in the company hierarchy. Understanding the fears, behaviours, and questions of all those concerned requires knowledge of the value systems of the company and the individual employees. With 9 levels, the current value systems of individuals, groups and organisations can be measured and the need for change can be presented based on numbers. 9 Levels enables the understanding of the ACTUAL situation as well as the definition of the TARGET situation for the desired corporate culture. The transparent presentation of the analysis makes it easy to understand and creates an ideal basis for further steps (in the form of consultation, training, or coaching) with the aim of reaching the desired TARGET situation.

Areas of application

Reasons for a cultural change:
- » More competitors enter the market
- » Customers can not be successfully retained
- » Good employees leave your company
- » Your company is not attractive for desperately needed specialists
- » Performance/productivity has declined
- » It is difficult to allow changes at the management level

Uses

The need for change is made visible and understandable. Mutual understanding between individuals as well as understanding for your company and its goals is awakened, thereby allowing for change. Your employees will feel understood and will voluntarily commit themselves to the company.

The cultural change will become the "driving force" for additional good employees / professionals and enhance the performance of the existing team who enjoy their jobs and feel understood and valuable. Your company can keep up with and surpass the competition and will learn how to be flexible in light of ever changing conditions.

Applications

A preliminarily assigned change team including you and other decision makers will participate in a workshop with a consultant/trainer/coach who is certified to work with 9 Levels and who will work through the value systems with the team. You will be sent a link with an access code to the 9 Levels online questionnaire in which you will fill out questions about the personal value system and the organisational value system. With the help of the evaluation (the report), you will receive a tangible, measurable statement about the level assigned to your company and the direction in which you should develop in order to implement typical recommendations and strategies for action.

Typical questions

» Why are we the way we are?

» Why is corporate culture so important, and how can it be changed?

» Can these changes be measured so that they can be better understood and controlled?

» How must we change in order to be able to survive in the market?

» What does cultural change mean for our employees?

» What do we need to do in order to "bring along" our employees?

» What should we do when we realise that one or more employees do not fit into our corporate culture?

Change processes

Situation & needs

The market is constantly evolving: the needs of customers are changing, new products and services must be introduced to the market, and internal structures are regularly reviewed. The constantly changing conditions require companies to be highly adaptable so that they can enter into tough competition with the front-runners.

Unfortunately, most business processes/change processes fail because they are set up too rationally or technically, i.e. the human side of change is ignored – the people and the culture are often forgotten.

Why 9 Levels?

9 Levels recognises the human side of change and creates acceptance amongst all employees. It makes value systems visible and tangible, thereby helping to answer important questions:

> » Is your organisation ready for the change process?
> » Which changes does your organisation require?

» In which direction must your organisation change in order to be successful?

» Or in some business sectors: is it perhaps simply a matter of expanding and optimising the current level of value culture in order to live up to the desires of your clients?

Areas of application

With 9 Levels, the values of individual people as well as teams/groups and entire organisations can be understood. On one hand, the value systems in your role as a decision maker should be recognised. The personal value system at the individual level with you as the decision maker will therefore be worked out.

In addition, a business survey can be conducted using the organisational value system in order to determine the ACTUAL situation and establish the direction in which your organisation should develop to achieve success in the long term.

Uses

9 Levels creates more transparency and security. It helps you to implement decisive strategies for change and reduce potential conflicts on the part of your employees. The desired changes can be adapted to the cultural values of your organisation and can therefore be realised more quickly and successfully. With 9 Levels, your employees will understand the change process and will be "brought along". In this way, they will contribute to the success of the company.

Applications

Your 9 levels consultant leads a workshop with you, the top management / decision makers in your company and proceeds to develop the individual levels of the value systems. Prior to this, he/she will have sent you a link with a code for the 9 Levels online questionnaire in which you and the other workshop participants will answer questions about the personal value system and the organisational value system. With the evaluation (the report), you and your consultant will obtain measurable statements about which level your organisation is at and in which direction you should develop in order to derive recommendations for action and to discuss the next steps.

Typical questions
» How can we make our organisation more binding, agile, and flexible?
» How do we manage to break the moderately functioning / non-functioning structures?
» How can we achieve efficient and successful teamwork?
» How do we achieve more participation? How do we manage to rekindle enthusiasm for the organisation?
» How should we approach the change so that it can be successful?

Individual coaching

Situation & needs

With the ever-increasing expectations in the business world and increasingly more complex challenges, there is also an increased demand for support in personal development, in the definition and implementation of objectives and in the sorting and structuring of thoughts and emotions. Coaching helps you regain clarity about individual situations and to identify ways to make your professional and personal life more satisfying.

Why 9 Levels?

With 9 Levels, the coaching process is transparent and tangible. It measures your value systems as well as those of the coachees and makes it easier for you and him/her to consciously deal with the current situation. The past and future can thereby be contemplated simultaneously: how you/your employees have fit into the company in the past and how the working environment/situation must be adapted in order to be able to act / react to the environment in a satisfactory and yet consistent and appropriate way. Because only then is it possible to be successful and happy.

Areas of application

- » Traditional individual coaching for personal challenges and for selected areas of development
- » Leadership consulting
- » Career guidance, placement/outplacement
- » From conflict coaching to team coaching
- » Project management coaching

Uses

The topic of values, which is often billed as "soft", becomes visible and tangible – and hence changeable. Especially those who are highly number-/data- or fact-oriented desire specific metrics in the coaching process. By making people aware of their own value systems, the process is set in motion – and this basis can always be used in the future.

Applications

You and/or the coachee will be sent a code for the 9 Levels online questionnaire in advance so you can complete the questions about the personal value system. The coach brings the evaluation of the questionnaire (the report) for the coaching session and discusses these with you or the clients. The report also includes some reflective questions that help you/the clients and the coach to come to a mutual understanding. Starting from the ACTUAL situation, both will jointly develop situational awareness and tailored development plans for a successful and happy future.

Typical questions

» Why am I currently stuck in this situation?

» What influence do my value systems have on my thoughts/feelings/actions?

» What are the differences between my value systems and those of my environment, company, management, and employees?

» How have my value systems developed/changed?

» What were the change-triggering events?

» How can the new working environment and tasks help me realise my full potential?

Leadership

Situation & needs

Leadership is clearly becoming more complex. Not only have the demands of companies and employees changed and increased over time, but so has the complexity of the tasks that need to be completed. This means that the demand for a new type of leadership has arisen – especially with respect to situation-adapted and employee-friendly leadership, which puts a specific individual focus on each company and which requires specialised skills. This is exactly where value-oriented leadership comes in.

Why 9 Levels?

9 Levels makes it clear why and how who should lead whom at which levels. Only when the leadership style, behaviour, and philosophy fit the employees, their value systems and the desired organisational

behaviour it is possible to collaborate successfully. Also, as a manager you can and will only be happy and successful if you behave both according to your own values and according to the values of the organisation that you manage. This is the only way to achieve the long-term goals of your team/department/organisation.

Areas of application

» In traditional leadership development where you will be sensitised to the different value systems that exist in organisations as well as in people and groups.

» In leadership consulting: how do career paths proceed? How should you behave when you encounter problems? How can you perform better across various reporting lines or corporate divisions?

» How should different employees be managed so that our goals can be achieved?

» In traditional individual coaching.

Uses

9 Levels brings additional value by creating awareness of value systems. It increases clarity and transparency and makes previously hidden things visible through scientifically proven measurement methods. It clarifies the past, the topics with which people might have problems, why people are unhappy with some topics, and which changes are meaningful and purposeful.

For leaders, the diversity of the employees will become clear – they will learn to lead in better and more individual ways and to optimally utilise resources. The result is an understanding of the importance of cultural values and their direct correlation with the success of the organisation.

Applications

You will be sent a code for the online questionnaire in which you will answer questions about the personal value system. Your trainer, coach, or consultant will then bring the report (the evaluation) to the next meeting and discuss the topics in the scope of the workshop, coaching, or training session. You will then work out how each level should be managed, which levels are harmonised more or less optimally with each other. You will also find concrete solutions for the implementation of leadership styles.

Typical questions

» At which level am I?
» What does my value system mean for my leadership?
» At which level are the employees that I manage?
» How must I adapt my management behaviour to them?
» How do I manage a heterogeneous team of people with differing value systems?
» How can I bring my personal leadership behaviour and the challenges of the organisation to a common denominator?

Outplacement/Placement

Situation & needs

The typical career paths which used to be very straightforward and stringent in the past are already outdated. Rather, flexibility and situational career counselling that adapts to the current needs of the employees as well as the company are in demand. This applies to positions within organisations as well as the search for ways in which an employee might feel more comfortable with his/her value systems.

Why 9 Levels?

With 9 Levels, the previous career path can be presented and this can be used to find out where employees can best be deployed based on their competencies and also whether job candidates meet the requirements of vacant positions and fit into the team they will be directly working with based on their value systems. 9 Levels provides answers to the questions that are important to the decision maker in the next steps: what is the value system of the applicant? What was important for him/her? What is currently important for him/her? What are his/her current value systems? Where does he/she see his/her development potential, where does he/she feel comfortable when making further career choices or seeking a new organisation?

Areas of application

Placement
- » Talent management
- » Career consulting
- » Youth executive career paths
- » To optimally use all long-standing employees and managers according to their strengths.

Outplacement
- » Dealing with the past: why is the current organisation no longer working? What has changed?
- » Which areas of activity would potentially be interesting?
- » Which organisations would be the right ones for the new area of activity?
- » Are there organisations in which the current duties could be carried out again?

Uses

9 Levels offers the advantage that it shows personal value systems in addition to the value systems of the organisation, department, and business area and how the value system of the (potential) employee fits in with all of these value systems. Everything that can be evaluated about past thus becomes a valuable wealth of experience. Building on this, together with the consultant/coach, solutions for the current situation can be found and intermediate- and long-term strategies can be developed.

Applications

The coachee/client is sent a code for the 9 Levels online questionnaire in which questions about the personal value system are answered. The consultant/coach brings this evaluation (report) to the next meeting. He then works through this report with the client to establish the value system and form hypotheses about the defining qualities of current and future organisational values so that a fit or congruency can be guaranteed. Together it will be worked out which tasks, departments, or companies best fit the client.

Typical questions

» Dealing with experiences: what experience have I had up to now? Which career moves have been excellent? In which situations did I feel comfortable? Were there trigger points or provoking situations in which I have changed or in which the organisation has changed? (e.g. a management change or a dramatic event resulting in altered values systems)

» Which value systems currently predominate in me, and which business environment would best suit me so that I can work successfully and contentedly?

Recruiting

Situation & needs

A big challenge for companies is filling open positions with the right employees. Many recruiting processes are limited to facts and expertise and do not give sufficient attention to human or personal factors.

Why 9 Levels?

Only those who feel comfortable at their place of work and whose value systems are congruent with those of the company are able to implement their competencies and perform well. Until now, it was quite difficult to grasp or even measure values. With 9 Levels, it is possible to measure and understand the value systems of employees and applicants, thereby including them into the selection process.

> » In which teams or departments does the (potential) employee fit?
> » Which properties should candidates bring for which position?
> » Which responsibilities are best suited for him/her, and which

are not?

» How can you get people to make long-term commitments to the company?

Areas of application

For individual recruiting via individual interview and the normal application procedures.

In career consulting and placement, when current employees apply for higher management or project responsibilities.

Uses

Your company will massively reduce the rate of recruitment errors and the selection process will be substantially easier. In addition, there is greater security in terms of putting the right employee in the right position, ensuring a better job satisfaction and a more successful and valuable employee for your company. This creates a higher degree of loyalty to the company. In addition, managers can more quickly achieve clarity about how employees should be managed.

Applications

Before the interview, the applicant will be sent a link to the 9 Levels online questionnaire. You and your employee/applicant will receive the evaluation (the report) on the personal value system and the organisational value system. The consultant analyses these value systems together with the employees/applicants. How well does he/she fit into the company? How well does he/she fit into the department? How well does he/she fit into the area of responsibility? Companies and applicants answer questions based on reflection and a comparison of value systems.

Typical questions

» How well does the employee/applicant fit in with us?

» Which tasks suit the employee/applicant?
» Will he/she be satisfied with/successful at this task?
» Will he/she be successful in meeting the challenges?
» To what extent can we rely on him/her or how congruent are our value systems?
» How well will the employee/applicant match the value systems and challenges of the organisation?

Team

Situation & needs

Teams and the configuration in which they work are decisive for the success of your business. The teams can generally be divided into four categories:

» A non-functioning team
» A well-functioning team
» An extremely well-functioning team
» A team that is still being assembled

The development of all four categories of teams can be strengthened and encouraged.

Why 9 Levels?

9 Levels makes it clear how the culture and relationships in a team structure should be so that the team can successfully meet challenges. With the help of 9 Levels, an ideal TARGET situation can be worked out based on the ACTUAL situation. Here, there is a huge difference

if the team at hand is a sales team that must take over a new market or if it's a research and development team that must first develop a new product and is quite distanced from the client. Alternatively, if you are a team in the property management of a large corporation, 9 Levels indicates which values systems and which culture is most appropriate for your team in your particular setting.

Areas of application

> Traditional team development measures in project work, in normal department work, in newly formed teams, and in poorly/well-functioning teams in order to continue to consolidate success.

> Process optimisation – also between two departments (here, collaborations can also be made transparent and measurable, and potential for conflict as well as ways to avoid it can be demonstrated).

> Traditional sales teams

Uses

9 Levels allows for the visualisation of value systems that were previously not transparent and shows the potential for change. With the group value system, your team culture can be measured with your value systems – and everything that can be measures can be used as a basis for the change process. The need for change will be made apparent to each team member, thereby facilitating general acceptance as well as implementation.

Applications

Each team member is sent a code and a link to the 9 Levels online questionnaire and answers questions regarding the group value system. The questions will address how he/she currently views his/her team and how the team works (view). Alternatively or additionally, a

TARGET view (how the team should optimally be) can be identified in order to determine how things should proceed.

In the workshop, your consultant/trainer/coach will discuss the various results with you and your team: an average result from the evaluation of the group value system reveals how the team is perceived by all team members. The individual observations of each team member show how each individual perceives the team. You will see that this results in a great need for discussion – regardless of whether the perspectives are different or similar. From this discussion, your consultant/trainer/coach then defines areas of development for your team (what should be changed, what should be discontinued, and/or what should be initiated) in order for your team to better meet its challenges.

Typical questions

- » How do we go about meeting our challenges?
- » Which value systems are relevant for us and the derived fields of action, and which attitudes are relevant?
- » Which team member plays which role?
- » Which team members would be best for which tasks?
- » Where should we place our values, which subject areas are less well defined? Which are very well defined?
- » How do we deal with the heterogeneity of the team? What opportunities arise from this, and where might conflicts arise?
- » Does this all fit with the challenges of the market and environment?

Distribution/sales

Situation & needs

The demands of the clients are increasing – this affects both the business-to-customer and business-to-business areas. Sales calls fail to meet the expectations of the clients just as standard solutions or emotionless marketing.

But which sort of client responds to which triggers? How can you recognise if you even concur with the end customer or business owner?

Why 9 Levels?

With 9 Levels, you will be able to better assess yourself as a sales rep. This allows for security and makes you open to understanding the client and his/her behaviour. In this way, you will learn how to reach and address your clients in a more target oriented manner.

Areas of application

Measurement of value systems in sales training:

» How does a sales rep carry out a value oriented client discussion, which includes everything from needs analysis to relationship building, to value proposition and objection handling/pretext treatment to completion and after sales?

» Value oriented price negotiations: Who needs what arguments? Who responds to which benefit arguments? What is important for whom? Who would like to be addressed in which manner?

» Complete value oriented sales processes: what product attributes, packaging, image, etc. does the product/service of your client need in order to be accepted on which level?

» "Loud brands" and "quiet brands": who is receptive to what? – so that your clients can establish their product portfolio accordingly.

Uses

Your salespeople can better understand the customer and their companies as well as the end users. Your sales reps can also better assess themselves and identify the clients that they can easily approach, the ones they find difficult, and above all, why this is the case. You recognise where your sales team can more readily achieve success and in which areas you may need to adjust because the market or customers have changed.

Applications

Before sales training, for example, your sales reps are sent a link with a code to the 9 Levels online questionnaire where they answer questions about their personal value system and/or the group value system. The consultant/trainer/coach brings the evaluation (the report) to the meeting and works through it in order to analyse the value systems and determine which value systems your primary contact/main customers have. Together with your sales reps, the consultant/trainer/coach will then work out how they can successfully serve, respond to, and consult your clients.

Typical questions

» Which challenges must my client meet and how can I support him/her in the process?
» Which value systems suit me or how do I typically behave?
» What is easy for me? With which values do I get on well?
» How can we set up our sales processes so that we can better comply with the wishes of customers (in terms of speed, flexibility, and individualisation)?
» How must we perform in the market in order to be successful? (Value-oriented marketing)

STORIES WRITTEN BY LIFE – THE 9 LEVELS ARE AMONG US ...

I have put down a few examples and stories for you that show how the 9 Levels are reflected in nearly any area of life.

The Olympic Games in the Focus of the 9 Levels

In modern times, the Olympic Games were introduced in 1894 as re-founding of the festival held in Olympia in Antiquity, based on the suggestion of Pierre Coubertin. As a "meeting of the world's youth", it was to serve athletic comparison and communication between peoples. This basic idea is very strong in the Green level. Looking at today's situation around Olympia, a critical viewer will find several colours - nearly like the Olympic rings: Green for the basic idea, Orange for competition and the will to win. Green also represents the Olympic idea of "the most important thing is taking part". Blue represents the controlling and regulating officers, referees and the safety staff. Red stands for manipulation, corruption and fraud, as well as doping. Yellow is for linking cultures, people and sports. Orange is found in marketing and Purple in the rituals and traditions around the basic idea of the torch run.

Blue and Orange Status Symbols

Blue and *Orange* like to use status symbols. *Blue* status symbols tend to be awarded officially and rather focus on the status to be shown. It conveys hierarchy and clarity in the system of order. *Orange* status symbols focus on the prestige and on what has been achieved. Of course, they can also be acquired on one's own in *Orange*.

Announced and Unannounced Radar Traps

Why are there warning signs in front of a radar trap on the road? Many drivers have wondered this thankfully but with some confusion. An American policeman once fittingly explained: "Our job is to slow down the traffic – not to make money". The *Blue* system wants to calm down traffic and make drivers drive more moderately, rather than ensuring that the investment made in the radar trap pays off as quickly as possible. Orange drivers often consider speed limits to be rather like well-intended advice or suggestions to point out the sense of a reference speed. They like to strategically drive just fast enough to maybe pay a hefty fine but keep their license. At 120, *Orange* will drive at around near 140, for example. *Orange* will be angry about the consistently correctly driving people in front of him as well - specifically if they drive on the left lane, thinking "They aren't allowed to go any faster here anyway."

Logistics from Orange to Green

In a trade company's workshop, I once witnessed an important statement by the logistics manager. The company is strongly driven by index figures. The areas of responsibility are always seen in comparison and every area manager tries to look as good as possible. Now, a 48-hours delivery was to be switched to a 24-hours delivery. This hugely worsened the costs of the logistics manager. He commented: "We need to learn that it is okay if one area becomes worse as long as it improves the overall result." He implicitly demanded the move from *Orange* to *Green* … Objectives were to be reached even better together.

Let's Quickly Save the World

In his song "nur noch kurz die Welt retten", Tim Bendzko sings a wonderful parody on the negative characteristics of the *Orange* high-speed business world: "I just need to quickly save the world, then I'll fly to you. Need to check 148,713 emails - who knows what else is going to happen to me, there's so much happening here."

Reinhard Mey's Annabelle

Singer-songwriter Reinhard Mey wrote many expressive songs - an exciting lyrical phrase from the point of view of the 9 Levels is found in his song, Annabelle. It is a homage to a partner who wants to live very unconventionally and thus rebels against the *Blue* bourgeois life. Many people who tend to think in absolute terms are strongly characterised by the *Blue level*. Mey sings: "You with your nonconformist uniform " – a nice description for Annabelle also being a *Blue* – just a different one. Many counter-movements and counter-attitudes are very *Blue* in their attitude.

Pretty Woman Goes Shopping

We have all often watched the love comedy Pretty Woman with Julia Roberts alias Vivian "Viv" Ward and Richard Gere alias Edward Lewis. I am referring to the beautiful scene when Vivian in her still "professional" outfit tries to buy bourgeois clothes at the Rodeo-Drive Boulevard and meets saleswomen who are very opposed to her. *Orange* Edward Lewis sends *Red* Vivian to buy *Blue/Orange* clothes. She goes to the Mecca of luxury shopping for this: the Rodeo Drive. The *Blue* saleswomen absolutely and very clearly reject her wishes. They do not wish to serve this customer. An *Orange* saleswoman would have asked the strangely clothed customer into a side room and sold her as much as possible. *Blue* won't do that. At the end of the movie, Edward Lewis changes from *Orange* towards *Green* when he realises that his company creates nothing permanent. He decides to build ships in future - large ships. His assistant Philip "Phil" Stuckey is rather *Red*.

Antiauthoritarian Education and What Happens When Children Start School ...

Putting it simply, anti-authoritarian education is targeted at not applying any rules in education to permit a child to fully develop and experience its abilities. The absoluteness of this concept has strong *Blue* characteristics already. Children were not given any rules or corrections. The child was virtually kept or blocked on the *Red level*. When entering school, however, the child enters a *Blue* system where it has to raise its hand before speaking, sit still for 45 minutes and comply with a great many rules. This offers potential for problems from the point of view of the 9 Levels.

Soccer is Our Life, King Soccer Rules the World!

"Fußball ist unser Leben, denn König Fußball regiert die Welt!" is the title of a popular song of the German soccer national team from 1974. Looking at today's professional soccer, it is a potpourri of many levels:

The competition in soccer generally is *Orange*, interrupted by *Red* fouls and hopefully controlled by *Blue* referees. Typical professional clubs often manifest as brought-together *Orange* teams which then lose against teams playing *Green*. *Red* officers assign the World Championship to the highest bidder behind the scenes. Soccer stadiums with their business lounges have *Orange* motivation - they are great business opportunities, which make the *Purple* fans angry. Just remember the furious speech of Uli Hoeneß, who was attacked by fans who complained about his capitalisation of soccer. Classic traditional clubs that are often found in the Ruhr area have loyal *Purple* fans that will stick with it through thick and thin. The "we're just as we are" faction is rather *Blue* in comparison. We must not forget the *Red* fan riots that are present nearly everywhere.

The Asian Fortune Cookie

Everyone knows the Asian fortune cookies. From the perspective of the 9 Levels, its origin is rather *Purple*, while today's tip-raising effect tends towards *Orange*. Depending on level distribution, people will believe in the text and message or not, which is a *Purple* feature.

8 Orange and 1 Blue in India

In a management workshop of a sales organisation in India, I performed a 9 Levels analysis with the Personal Value System. The objective was to improve the understanding for each other within the management team and to achieve better team work. The main alignment of eight of the nine managers was *Orange*. Only one had *Blue* as his main alignment. They quickly wanted to know who had this *Blue* main alignment. The head of administration and accounting raised his hand. Enthusiastically and thankfully, the *Orange* managers now understood the accurate and correct action and thinking of their colleague, who in turn promised after the workshop to show better understanding for the *"Oranges"* in future. The parent group, interestingly, is rather *Blue* in its structure, but the Indian sales organisation was characterised *Orange* from the time of its founding.

A Manager Riding His Harley on the Weekend

There are some unparalleled cult companies, and Harley-Davidson is one of them. The motorcycle producer from Milwaukee has a cult and slightly wicked reputation. Rockers and bikers love the brand and the connected lifestyle. True Harley riders have internalised this philosophy in life and may be organised in clubs as well. These clubs are reminiscent of tribes and clans with a *Purple level* and *Red occurrences*. The hobby Harley riders like to get on their expensive bike after work or on weekends. Among them are many well-earning *Orange* managers that like to put on robes or Harley jackets to ride around as a *Red* terror or raise attention with illegally Red exhausts. Bikers also call this the A-jacket, a black Harley jacket with an *Orange* breast thing – every a… has one.

This is how the Harley enthusiasts are divided into true and wanna-be tribe members. This is how the *Orange* manager shows that he is only a hobby biker even by his colour choice.

Christmas – A Celebration of Love and Levels

Christmas shopping in Dubai. In the Advent days before Christmas, I once was at a management congress in Dubai. I was shocked at how dominant the commercial Christmas shopping is used in this originally Arab country. Christmas shopping in New York seems more logical. Surveys about Christmas regularly show how few people still know about the actual reason of why we celebrate Christmas.

Rituals and traditions are raised up high at Christmas. The traditional Christmas meal, always the same ceremony that must not be changed ever and that may lead to interesting discussions when families merge and cannot devise on the proper Christmas food. Clerical Christmas is a classically *Blue* subject celebrated with many *Purple* rituals and traditions. Some family members, however, cannot stand these *Purple* rituals and then escape in *Red* to do what they want to do. The other family members tend to not take this very well.

Children of Entrepreneurs Found Companies More Often

Statistically, entrepreneurs' children are more likely to found companies of their own than others. The early characterisation of these children in discussions at the table, on the weekend and on "what Mama and Papa do on their jobs" does leave a mark. The living circumstances characterise value systems. Children of *Blue* employees tend in *Blue* groups to go to those as well, where they are safe and well-cared for. *Orange* households in contrast tend to give birth to *Orange* founders. However, statistically seen, the third generation of entrepreneur children tends to run into unmoving walls with their companies. They are often lacking entrepreneurial competence as well as *Orange* will.

Orange Risk Athletes and Red Daredevils

Extreme athletes are often said to be potential suicides. *Red* extreme athletes will not think about consequences. They merely act and break limits and rules. They truly live a high-risk life. *Orange* extreme athletes believe in surpassing borders and in general feasibility. They are driven by the wish of moving borders. In contrast to the *Reds*, however, they invest lots of time and energy in minimising and controlling risk. Flight pioneer and balloon world record holder Steve Fossett once said that he was not looking for risk - he invested most energy into minimising risk.

THERMALS FOR THE VALUE SYSTEMS

A report on the mental preparation for the World Cup

How can man/woman prepare optimally for a World Championship if the goal is to score as successfully as possible in the individual as in the team ranking? Which mental aspects play a role here, how do the value systems of individual pilots affect their behaviour and action in the group?

In order to get answers to these questions, Dörte Starsinski, spokeswoman of the German National Glider Team, organised a workshop with me on 3rd March 2013 in Frankfurt. The aim of the workshop was to gain clarity about the importance of mental processes and value systems in order to prepare even more precisely and purposefully for the 2013 World Cup in Issodoun, France.

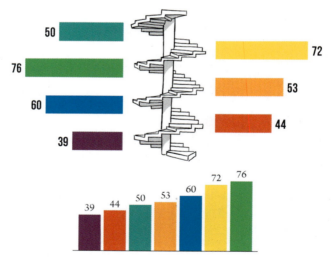

Personal Value System – ACTUAL (Average)
German National Glider Team Women

"The 9 Levels of Value Systems"

The "9 Levels of Value Systems", a scientifically valid model for measuring value systems in individuals (Personal Value System), groups (Group Value System) and organisations (Organisation Value System), was used as the central model. In doing so, both the ACTUAL state can be recorded as well as a TARGET to be striven for. In the case of the glider a combination of both possibilities made sense.

In the run-up to the workshop, the participants were given the task of completing three 9 level questionnaires online, which included different perspectives:

» How am I as a glider pilot in competition? (Personal - ACTUAL)
» How should I be as a glider pilot in competition if I want to become world champion? (Personal - TARGET)
» How do we have to function as a group if we want to be very successful? (Group - TARGET)

The model is quite complex at first glance and can be explained very quickly and easily on closer inspection. Each level of the dynamic model represents its own level of development. The respective value system determines the way of thinking and behaving. There are basically two sides in the model, the right side of the I reference and the left side of the WE-reference. In the first case I try to adapt the world to myself, while in the second case the development takes place by adapting to my changed environment. Each system - whether person, group or organisation - passes through the levels in sequence from bottom to top, whereby it is not possible to skip a level. What is important is that it is not a question of "the higher the better", but rather of the matching or congruence of the value systems to the challenges of the living world. So a glider pilot at a world championship certainly needs a different value system than a kick boxer in a ring. The need for change is always there when the challenges of the living world can no longer be mastered at the current stage of development. More complex problems require more complex thinking structures and solutions.

Christine Grote, world champion in the club class, over 9 levels: "The seminar definitely made my life more colorful. The different levels of the 9 levels and their colors make my value system clearer, more tangible and in part only recognizable. And as an old German proverb says: "Knowledge is the first step to recovery." Of course, each further step means work on myself, but after many other approaches I find something in the contents of the workshop that suits me personally and will certainly allow me to progress. And who knows, maybe the confrontation with 9 levels and the inner teams also brings the chance to get ahead with other concepts, e.g. scripts for the first time".

Levels for gliding

How can these levels of the model's value systems be transferred to the glider world? The lowest level (Beige) doesn't really matter, here it's only about the livelihood. With Purpur rituals are lived (keyword: "admission into the witch alliance"), custom care, superstition in aviation as well as strong rootedness in the homeland. The red glider pilot does his thing, acts impulsively, wants to be the greatest and is not very considerate. At Blau, rules, structures, quality assurance and also the club dairy are added. Everything is perfectly organised and strictly regulated; in its negative form over-regulated. Orange is goal-oriented, believes in the feasibility of technology, is downright driven and always wants to achieve more. When it comes to green, the real TEAM idea comes to the fore, you see that you can achieve even more together with Orange's goal orientation. Long-term success, dialogue and human relations are important to the green glider pilot. While Orange may not pass on some of the information to his team mates, this is a matter of course for Green. Red would deliberately send out misinformation in order to gain a personal advantage and harm the others. Yellow adds a multi-perspectivity that is hidden from the previous levels. The combination of knowledge, the constant increase in knowledge, flexibility and independence are just as important as systemic thinking, the ability to think abstractly, networks and changing cooperations.

How these value systems are distributed among the pilots and how they should be distributed in order to be successful was examined on the basis of the survey with 9 levels.

Sue Kussbach, who won her third World Championship title, explained: "I became curious about the 9 levels system. I will take this aspect into account in my World Cup preparations."

Implementing in competition

The results of the surveys showed a very clear relevance of the green and yellow levels in the main characteristics, coupled with a blue reliability and perfect organization in the entire squad. In the workshop we worked out what this means for the whole team as a group and for each individual during a World Cup. A central point was the focus on the value systems of the World Cup and also how influences from other areas of life (professional, private, etc.) can be controlled and faded out during this time.

Conny Schaich, Vice World Champion in the Standard Class, commented the workshop as follows:

"It is very valuable for me to have got to know the 9 levels for the upcoming World Championship flights. It helps you to understand and classify your own behaviour patterns as well as those of your team partners or trainers. With this basis I would like to try to work out starting points before the World Cup, which can help me with a successful result".

In the aftermath of the workshop, the national men's team was questioned by team supervisor Gaby Haberkern. It was interesting to see that the value systems are forming differently and that some of the gentlemen have different priorities.

The key to success in top-class sport

The Blue Level is more important for the men. Clear rules and structures as well as order and quality assurance seem to be more important here than with their female colleagues.

Katrin Senne, third in the 15m class:
"What was interesting for me was the 9 levels value system: Where do I stand in relation to the World Cup and where the team stands - and where should we develop as a team? And that this system can be applied and explained to so many life situations. Politics, state systems and business."

The outstanding achievements at this world championship of female glider pilots show that working with value systems and mental models is also an important success factor in top-class sport. Those who are aware of their values and value systems and can optimally adapt them to the given challenges will be more successful in the long term. In a manner of speaking: thermals for the value systems.

The ladies of the national gliding team rated the workshop with Rainer Krumm (right) very positively.

RAINER KRUMM – THE EXPERT FOR THE 9 LEVELS

Rainer Krumm is a management trainer, consultant and coach. He studied business education and strategic management and supported, consulted, trained and coached international companies, top executives and teams in more than 23 countries. He is deemed one of the most experienced international consultants and trainers in the area of corporate culture and change management and bases his approach on the developmental psychology of Prof. Clare W. Graves.

He is the founder and manager of axiocon GmbH, a corporate consulting firm specialising in organisational & value management.

Rainer Krumm is also the founder and chairman of the 9 Levels Institute for Value Systems GmbH & Co. KG – an institute that develops and sells the scientifically secured and practice-tested analysis tools for the model of 9 Levels.

The institute, which is headquartered in Ravensburg, Germany specialises in the development and sale of analysis tools for value systems. It performs scientific examinations and further developments on the model of 9 Levels of Value Systems.

The institute also offers certifications for consultants, trainers and coaches who want to supplement and enrich their daily work with the analysis tools of the 9 levels.

Contact: info@9levels.com | www.9levels.com

REFERENCES

Bär-Sieber, M., Krumm, R., Wiehle, H.; *Unternehmen verstehen, gestalten verändern – Das Graves-Value-System in der Praxis*, Gabler Verlag, Wiesbaden, 3rd extended edition, 2015

Beck, D. E., Cowan, C. C., *Spiral Dynamics – Mastering Values, Leadership and Change*, Blackwell Publishing, Williston 1996

Bucksteeg, Mathias, Hattendorf, Kai, *Wertekommission Führungskräftebefragung*, Bonn, 2012

Dobbelstein, T., Krumm, R., *9 Levels for Value systems - Development of a scale for level-measurement*, in: Journal of Applied Leadership and Management 07-2012

Graves, C. W., *The Implications to Management of System – Ethical Theory*, o.O., 1962

Graves, C. W., *Value System And Their Relation to Managerial Controls And Organizational Viability*, Schenectady, 1965

Graves, C. W., Huntley, W. C., LaBier, D. W., *Personality Structure and Perceptual Readiness; An Investigation of Their Relationship to Hypothesized Levels of Human Existence*, Schenectady, 1965

Graves, C. W., *Deterioration of Work Standards*, Harvard Business Review, 44 (September/October, 1966), S. 117-128

Graves, C. W., *Levels of Existence: An Open System Theory of Values*, in: Journal of Humanistic Psychology, Alameda, Volume 10 (Fall, 1970), No. 2, S. 131-155

Graves, C. W., Madden H.T.; Madden, L.P., *The Congruent Management Strategy*, o.O. 1970

Graves, C. W., *How Should Who Lead Whom to do What?*, YMCA Management Forum, Schenectady, 1971-1972

Graves, C. W., *Human Nature Prepares for a Momentous Leap*, The Futurist, Bethesda, No. 8, April, 1974, pp. 72-87

Graves, C. W., *Summary Statement: The Emergent, Cyclical, Double-Helix Model of Adult Human Biopsychosocial Systems, Boston*, 1981

Graves, C. W., *Levels of Human Existence* (transcript from a seminar), edited by W.R. Lee, Santa Barbara, ECLET, 2002

Graves, C. W., *The Never Ending Quest*; edited by Ch. Cowan and N. Todorovic, Santa Barbara, ECLET, 2005

Krumm, R., *Coaching mit den 9 Levels*, in: Coaching heute, Munich, 07-2012

Krumm, R., *Steht klassisches Training schon bald vor dem Untergang?*, in: Zukunft Training, Munich, 07-2012

Krumm, R., Parstorfer, B.; Clare W. Graves: His Life and his Work, iUniverse, Bloomington, 2018

Lee, B., *Transcription of a „Seminar on Levels of Human Existence"* conducted by Dr. Graves at the Washington School of Psychiatry, October 16, Washington, 1971

Lipkowski, S., *Neun Stufen der Entwicklung*, in: trainingaktuell, 05-2012

Tad, J.; Woodsmall, W., *Time Line*, Paderborn, Junfermann Verlag, Paderborn, 1991

RAINER KRUMM & BENEDIKT PARSTORFER

CLARE W. GRAVES:
HIS LIFE AND HIS WORK

"This book, an outstanding work by co-authors Rainer Krumm and Benedikt Parstorfer, is an important contribution to preserve, spread and further adapt Graves' work."

—**DON BECK** (Co-Author of "Spiral Dynamics")

CLARE W. GRAVES
HIS LIFE AND HIS WORK

No one has influenced our understanding of culture and value systems as much as Clare W. Graves, US American professor of social psychology and originator of the emergent theory of human development. His relevance to the field of consulting and organizational development is indisputable. However, only few authors have dealt with Graves' original data.

This book is the worldwide first summary of Graves' original studies, audiotapes, and notes, as well as a complete biography and comprehensive explanation of its scientific relevance in regard to human development.

Rainer Krumm and Benedikt Parstorfer's intent is to spread the knowledge and wisdom of Graves and his extensive studies and offer the interested reader a thorough understanding of his original work and various applications.

> *"This book, an outstanding work by co-authors Rainer Krumm and Benedikt Parstorfer, is an important contribution to preserve, spread and further adapt Graves' work."*
>
> —**DON BECK** (Co-Author of "Spiral Dynamics')

Author: Rainer Krumm

ISBN: 978-1532038433

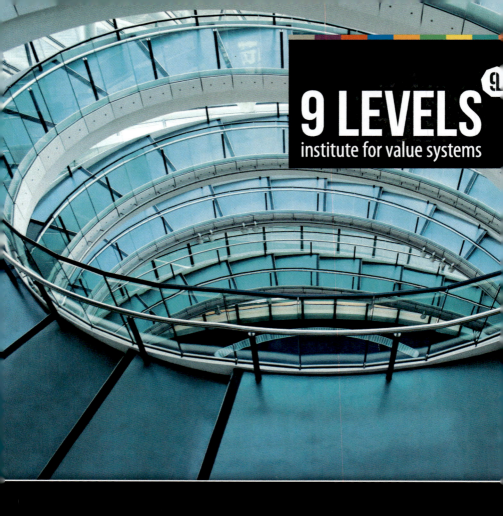

THE 9 LEVELS INSTITUTE FOR VALUE SYSTEMS

9 LEVELS INSTITUTE FOR VALUE SYSTEMS GMBH & CO. KG
Eywiesenstraße 6 | 88212 Ravensburg | Germany
T +49 751 363 44-999 | F -739 | info@9levels.com | www.9levels.com

The 9 Levels Institute for Value Systems is a consulting institute that is specialized in the measurement and analysis of value systems of persons, groups, organizations and systems. Scientifically well-founded and reliable in practice – that is our credo.

Founder Rainer Krumm contributes his experience from change projects in more than 23 countries and 57 different nationalities.

Corporate cultures and team cultures are the key to sustainably successful companies. The corporate culture can be measured and, if required, changed to last. This is not a simple way – but it is manageable.

Many different management influences and the development theory of Prof. Dr. Clare W. Graves have been included in model development. They were alway subjected to reviews for their suitability for practical application. From users for users – this is the only way in which projects and measures can be successful. Whether we like it or not, the world increasingly changes.

Corporate flexibility is a central factor for the future. This needs to be secured by value analyses and change actions where applicable.

Many tools start with unchangeable typologies or behavioural orientation. According to our conviction and experience, measures that are successful in the long term are aligned with values – the values of the actors and the values shared in the group.

Every company has its corporate culture. Only very few are aware of it.